Mourning
Song

Mourning Song

Joyce Landorf Heatherley

Fleming H. Revell
A Division of Baker Book House Co
Grand Rapids, Michigan 49516

© 1974, 1994 by Joyce Landorf Heatherley

Published by Fleming H. Revell
a division of Baker Book House Company
P.O. Box 6287, Grand Rapids, MI 49516-6287

Printed in the United States of America

Library of Congress Cataloging-in-Publication Data

Heatherley, Joyce Landorf
    Mourning song.
      ISBN 0-8007-5547-2
    1. Death. I. Title.
    BT825.L35 248'.86   74-9938

Unless otherwise indicated, Scripture references are from *The Living Bible,* copyright © 1971 by Tyndale House Publishers, Wheaton, Illinois. Used by permission.
    Scripture marked KJV is taken from the King James Version of the Bible.
    Scripture marked MLB is taken from the MODERN LANGUAGE BIBLE: THE BERKELEY VERSION IN MODERN ENGLISH. Copyright © 1945, 1959, 1969 by Zondervan Publishing House. Used by permission.
    Scripture marked RSV is taken from the Revised Standard Version of the Bible, copyright 1946, 1952, 1971, and 1973 by the Division of Christian Education of the National Council of the Churches of Christ in the United States of America.
    Excerpts from ON DEATH AND DYING by Elisabeth Kübler-Ross (Copyright © 1969 by Elisabeth Kübler-Ross) are used by permission of the publishers, Macmillan Publishing Co., Inc., New York.
    "A Psalm on the Death of an 18-Year-Old Son" is from *Psalms of My Life* by Joseph Bayly, Tyndale House Publishers, Wheaton, Illinois. Used by permission.
    "The Sound of Music" is from THE SOUND OF MUSIC © Copyright 1959 by Richard Rodgers and Oscar Hammerstein II. Williamson Music, Inc., New York, N.Y., owner of publicational and allied rights for all countries of the Western Hemisphere. All Rights Reserved. Used by permission.
    "The Grandfather" by Robert M. Howell is reprinted from THE CHRISTIAN by permission of The Christian Board of Publication, St. Louis.
    Excerpts from THE RICHEST LADY IN TOWN by Joyce Landorf, Copyright © 1973 by the Zondervan Corporation are used by permission.
    Poems "Remembered Sin," "Teach Me to Walk Alone," "The Heart Held High," "Broken Dreams," "Remembered Dreams," "Friends," and "The Other Side," by Martha Snell Nicolson are from *Her Best for the Master* copyright 1964, Moody Press, Moody Bible Institute of Chicago. Used by permission.
    "The False Friends," by Dorothy Parker, Introduction by Brendan Gill is from THE PORTABLE DOROTHY PARKER Copyright 1928, renewed ©1956 by Dorothy Parker. Used by permission of Viking Penguin, a division of Penguin Books USA Inc.
    "Go Down Death—A Funeral Sermon" is from GOD'S TROMBONES by James Weldon Johnson. Copyright 1927 by The Viking Press, Inc., renewed © 1955 by Grace Nail Johnson. Used by permission of Viking Penguin, a division of Penguin Books USA Inc.

This book is lovingly dedicated to

Von Letherer

A man who has courageously faced and coped with death
and dying for all of his years.

His life as a dauntless Christian and his remarkable silence
through the years of pain-filled illness have honed and refined
him into a dangerously beautiful, Christlike man. The song
of mourning constantly swirls about him, yet the clear, ringing, dolce melody of Christ's love is never lost or obscured.
In hearing the spirited bravura of this man's music, our hearts
have been lifted toward Christ and we have been deeply
touched—we will never be the same again!

Contents

Acknowledgments

My thanks to
Brenda Arnold, Wendy Justice, and Connie Giles

For the song you lovingly played on your typewriter—including both the rough draft and the final manuscript of this book—I thank you! Such talent!

Preface

As I see it, the differences between two people having a face-to-face conversation and one person reading another's printed words are far more distinct than I once imagined. In a conversation I can look into your eyes. I can tell whether they twinkle, tear up, harden, or withdraw. I can hear each inflection in your voice, which allows me to glimpse the true essence of your heart. Perhaps more importantly, in a conversation, if you don't understand my words or you misinterpret my meaning, I can quickly backtrack and set things right by saying, "Oh, no, that's not what I meant." Sensing your dismay or pain, I can say, "Oh dear, I'm sorry. I didn't mean to offend you . . . forgive me."

When, as a writer, I attempt to communicate with you, my readers, well, that's quite a different story and a one-sided one at that. Reading isn't a conversation, no matter how gifted or insightful the author may be.

Once I've finished writing and the book is published, I go through a few tormented months fretting over what I wrote and how I expressed myself. During this period I agonize, "Oh dear, I wish I'd written about *this!* I wish I'd had the skill to say *that* more astutely!"

With these thoughts in mind, you can imagine how surprised, honored, and delighted I was when William Petersen, editorial director of Revell, requested I update and revise

Mourning Song for a new paperback edition. His request brought me joyous relief: Here was my chance to rewrite, to smooth out, to add or delete text in some roughly written passages. In short, a chance to say, "Here's what I really meant, and here's what I've learned."

Best of all, rewriting gives me the opportunity to include almost thirty years of conversations and experiences I've had with many of you. I'm extremely grateful to you wonderful readers who came forward after *Mourning Song* was first published in 1974 to share your own struggles, joys, doubts, victories, questions, and amazing stories of how God and his people comforted you and gave you strength as you walked along the arduous path in the valley of the shadow of death.

Valuing your contributions, dear readers, remembering my own walk during these past decades, and being keenly aware of the place where I stand now with the terrible and beautiful gift of cancer in my life, I eagerly begin this writing and pray with all my heart:

Dear Lord,

Take my pen and write for all of us some fresh bright lessons from our pain and suffering. Prescribe bold and strong messages of hope from our tragic and seemingly endless parade of losses.

Give us, once again, not only the courage to move from one day to the next but also new visions that we may dream again within our hearts.

So that no matter the length or breadth of our days, our lives will shine with your love, grace, and forgiveness; and when all is said and done, we will make you proud that we are your children.

1

The Appointment

And as it is appointed unto men once to die.

Hebrews 9:27 KJV

Long before I knew anything about reading a calendar, arranging schedules, or keeping appointments, I knew about music.

Singing, playing the piano, and listening to music, both at home and at church, color most of my childhood memories in lovely, warm shades of rose and peach. Now, almost sixty years later, my heart is still touched by the colors and sounds of music-past, which permeated my life, but the colors are a little faded.

As I grew up, I discovered there was one song I didn't want to sing: the song of mourning. When called upon, I could sing it for others but not for me. In fact, I planned to sing it only in the hazy, distant future. I pushed the melody and lyrics of mourning songs as far out of my head and heart as possible and prayed, "Please God, don't ask me to sing any of *those* songs . . . at least not until I'm very old."

However, those plans, which sounded perfectly rational to me at the time, were not based on the realities of life and death. Several events in the 1960s severely rattled the cages of my mind, and I found myself singing the songs of mourning in spite of all my wishful thinking and denial. I emerged from the '60s and went shakily into the '70s. I was full of painful memories, unexplained emotions, and unmentionable fears from the deaths of my loved ones.

But the events that had rattled my cages in the '60s were like mild tremors compared to the next two decades of seismic earthquakes, which I never saw coming. I've always heard that trauma and unexplainable losses almost always come in bunches. What I didn't know was that they could come each year or each decade. To my utter horrified amazement, I was to discover that the '70s would be no better than the '60s. I found myself deluged with grief and mourning songs, only this time the "events" were unbearable physical and emotional pain.

Then, even worse than the events of the previous decades, the '80s produced a whole new holocaust in my little corner in the world. Does any of this sound familiar to you? Have you, as I, been known to stumble around in some kind of emotionally dense fog mumbling, "I can't believe this is happening! What's coming up next? Does the pain ever go away? This has been so unreal I think I'm losing my mind."

Mourning songs at this point for me were almost deafening; and instead of refusing to hear them, since I had very little choice, I changed directions and tried to force my appointment with death. I wanted to sing those sad, angry songs and be done with this life, which had started out in such beautiful shades of rose and peach but now had become tarnished with the grayish-brown stain of death.

Then, just at the end of the '80s, it looked as if God were going to give me a vacation from catastrophic events. I felt a measure of sadness lifting from my soul, as if God had taken his artist brushes and had begun to paint in broad strokes the colors of Easter across the canvas of my soul. I began to breathe again. I was leaving Calvary and moving toward the resurrection garden. I slipped back into familiar habits and thought patterns, and with the past events and lessons firmly under my belt, I began to sing the old trusted songs of faith, of grace, and of God's love. This period of grace was violently interrupted and obliterated by one of my worst three fears coming dreadfully true.

In my speaking engagements over the last few years, I've casually mentioned that, while I had experienced a lot of painful events, I hadn't suffered from the big, scary ABC's: Alzheimer's, bankruptcy, or cancer. There have been days that I, at sixty-one years of age, was sure I detected the onset of Alzheimer's. Since Francis Heatherley and I started our publishing company, I've wondered a few times how close we were to falling off the hazardous cliffs of bankruptcy. And, of course, there's my family history of cancer. But, perhaps like you, I didn't believe these things would actually camp on my doorstep any time soon.

Now, barely into the '90s, the time has come for my own appointment with breast cancer. The haunting melodies of mourning throb in my soul; I hear them as they begin to emerge from my throat.

Perhaps like you, I simply did not anticipate that any of the events and dire circumstances of those three decades would happen to *me*. To others? Yes. To you? Probably. To *me*? I don't think so. Sure, I knew realistically, way down deep inside me, that it is "appointed unto men once to die"; but had you and I talked about the "when" of the dying, I would probably have laughed and assured you it wouldn't be for a long, long time.

In the past I had given my own dying a passing thought or two; but I was not convinced, given the press of daily living, that the whole subject of my death was worth my consideration to any significant degree. In short, I never wanted to face it or deal with it—any time soon.

I was like an army general whom I met while I was singing and speaking at a military base. We were having dinner and discussing some important issues of life when he said something about letting his wife handle all religious or spiritual areas of their life for both of them.

"What would happen, General," I asked, "if for some reason you had a heart attack tonight, and when you asked your doctor to level with you about your progress, he told you that you might not live the day out? Would you be content to let your wife handle all spiritual subjects, or would you take matters into your own hands and go directly to God?"

He put both elbows on the table, rested his chin in his hands, and looked at me for a long time. Finally, he said, "Honey, I've just never given any thought to death, especially my own, and frankly, no one has ever asked me such a question."

I thought, *I can see how that's entirely possible.* Built-in death denial comes as easily to us as breathing. *Why be worried?* we think. *Why not just take death and dying when and where it comes? Why make out a will? Why talk of our wishes concerning our funeral? Why talk of death (ours or someone else's) when it's so sad and depressing?* Goodness knows, we don't want to be accused of being morbid or depressed!

Why indeed? Part of the answer lies in the unnerving fact that no matter how well prepared we are to face death, it always catches us unawares and at the worst possible moment. It is usually brutal except when we become willing to learn from the dying. Then it is just a little less brutal.

Even now I would like to put off writing this book. Yet the events I describe have produced ongoing results in the quality of my life. They have brought a large measure of meaning to my daily living. I must not ignore the voices of these events, even though the lessons they've taught me concern some of the most powerful fears of anyone's life—death and dying.

The first of my appointments with death happened in 1964. My son, Rick, was twelve years old; my daughter, Laurie, just ten. To my great surprise, I became pregnant, and after eight months of the most difficult pregnancy I'd ever experienced, I had a C-section surgery and gave birth to a baby boy. I named him David, after my favorite: David, the sweet, gifted singer of the Psalms.

The nurse said, "If you want to see a beautiful baby, turn your head to the left." I did, and there he was. His eyes angelic sky blue and his head covered with fine, corn silk–golden hair. For me, it was instantaneous love just to look at him.

I never found out if David would sing as his famous namesake had because he took one look around, thought about it for one long day, and went straight back to God without a backward glance. I didn't even get to hold him or tell him good-bye.

Months later I was still wandering in the wilderness of grief, utterly devastated. I tried to find my way out, without letting too many people know I was lost, but the maps I read were filled with sticky-sweet poems and unreal directions. All the streets came to dead ends.

In 1965, one year after David's funeral, my Aunt Grace called me. She said my darling Grandpa Uzon had felt chest pains that morning. He had awakened her and then calmly returned to his living room in the little house behind hers to wait for the doctor and EMTs.

By the time help arrived, Grandpa had caught his flight home and was winging his way upward. I didn't get to say good-bye to him, either.

When no one close to you has ever died, and then two loved ones are taken in one year, you feel just like Humpty Dumpty. You've fallen off the wall and you know all the king's horses and all the king's men are never going to be able to put you together again.

Having two loved ones die one year apart did not in any way prepare me for a third death in 1966. Nine months after I sang for Grandpa's funeral, I had to surrender my fifty-seven-year-old mother to the waiting arms of God.

I remember I was utterly exhausted with waiting and watching around the clock for seven weeks at UCLA Medical Center. My husband, Dick Landorf, phoned me and told me I should come home and sleep in my own bed, that my children needed me. I drove home and was in bed no more than a few hours when death played the meanest trick of all: It took her and I didn't even get to see her go. Again, I didn't get to say good-bye.

The next months were the most puzzling times of my life. Every once in a while I would have marvelous, incredible moments with God. His ability and power to comfort me temporarily brought miraculous relief. But these moments were most often followed by weeks where I felt absolutely alone. It seemed as if someone waved a magic wand and God simply disappeared. My grief, my loneliness, sometimes my anger, welled up and gushed over the top of me. No matter how hard or how long I yelled, God did not seem to hear me.

I was in the dressing room of a TV studio when a woman recognized me. She'd read my books and asked if I was writing another. When I told her yes and said that it was about death and dying, she replied almost casually, "Oh, I lost my teenage daughter a few years ago." I asked her if she would mind telling me about it. She assured me not only wouldn't she mind talking about it, but also she would be quite happy to. So she related the doctor's diagnosis of cancer in her seventeen-year-old daughter, the months of illness, and finally, the girl's death.

I couldn't imagine how heavy the weight of grief would be in this mother, so I asked, "Tell me, how did you cope with your grief after your daughter died?"

"Oh, my dear" she said, looking a bit surprised at my question, "I didn't *have* any grief. None at all. God took it *all* away from me."

Now, I love God with all my heart, and I was quite sure this woman did too, but what had she done that I had failed to do? Or why had God done this for her and not for me? I rephrased the question: "Go back to when you were told by the doctors that your daughter had cancer, before she died, how did you handle the grief of *that* news?"

She stared at me for a second or two and said, "I've already told you. God took away my grief. I didn't have any grief. In fact, I didn't even shed a tear."

Long after the lady left I stood there thinking, *No tears? How can that be?* The many months of grief, tears, anger, and fragmentation I'd experienced after the deaths of my baby, my grandfather, and my mother came vividly to mind.

After hearing how God dealt with that woman, I wondered if I would ever be able to understand anything about death. I wondered if God played favorites, and if he did, how could he?

Then God used (of all things!) *Life* magazine to answer me. Just before the '60s came to an end, an exciting article appeared in *Life*. Written by the brilliant and sensitive Dr. Elisabeth Kübler-Ross, this short but thought-provoking article answered some of the questions about death and dying that plagued me.

After reading that article, I realized it was not a cardinal sin to cry over the loss of a loved one. It was not a sin or even a crime to feel anger and other emotions that ravaged one's soul. In fact, it was normal. I was normal. I was *not* grieving because God had failed me or was silent or because I had been untrue to him and was somehow spiritually deficient or dysfunctional as a Christian. I was suffering the grief process because as a mother, a granddaughter, and a daughter, I longed to be with my baby, my grandfather, and my mother. Oh, how I missed them—and I find after all these years I still do.

Dr. Kübler-Ross wrote of five emotional stages terminal patients experience once they know they are going to die. The first is denial, then anger, bargaining, depression, and finally, acceptance. Dr. Kübler-Ross gained her knowledge

by talking with over two hundred terminally ill patients, and
the results of her research were compiled in her book *On
Death and Dying.*

I was stunned by the truth of the article, since I'd watched
all of those stages in my mother; but I was even more fascinated by the fact that in my bereavement I had identified
with each and every stage, as did all the members of my family. Some stages I had repeated, and one I had skipped . . .
but only temporarily.

My whole family went through denial, anger, bargaining,
and depression into acceptance and then back again to repeat
some stages. Later, as I read Dr. Kübler-Ross's whole book,
it stirred my soul toward facing the realities of not only the
deaths of others but my own dying as well.

Reading that book also marked the beginning of my most
spiritually soul-searching times before God. I went back to
the Bible. Answers that had been invisible before clearly began
to surface on the pages. For the first time in two years, I found
workable techniques to slow the flow of my hemorrhaging
grief.

I am not writing about these experiences out of a medically or scientifically acquired knowledge, although I have
read extensively and talked with some of the finest professionals in medicine. I am not a doctor.

Neither do I write about coping with death and dying from
a theological position, although I believe Jesus Christ is the
Son of God, the very one who died using his own life and
body as a sacrifice for my sins. I have asked him into my life,
and I am joyous at being known as a Christian. But I am not
a minister.

I am not writing as a trained professional either, although
I have worked with some of America's most gifted psychologists. I am not a psychologist, counselor, social worker, or
grief therapist.

I write these thoughts from the feeling level of my own
heart and from the feeling level of thousands of conversa-

tions with others who were thrown either violently or slowly into the grief process.

A friend once said, "If there is to be an honest approach to death it must be with childlike feeling. It must be couched and surrounded by trust, honesty, and openness." It is that feeling level of our souls that death chooses to make its most accurate bull's-eye. No one faced with his or her own imminent death, sitting by the dying, or identifying a loved one's body in the morgue has ever escaped death's penetrating message.

I admit I didn't enjoy learning the messages about death. I don't like growing pains any more now than I did when my bones ached with growth during my adolescent development. If my experience has taught me any lesson well, however, it's that if we ever stop learning and become arrogant know-it-alls, we stop being alive to life.

I am not writing this book to a select few. It would be unrealistic to write it only for bereaved parents, a grieving child, a shattered teenager, or a floundering widow. Death is a very real part of our daily living and comes to every person. As surely as we are born, death comes to all of us.

Putting our heads ostrich-style in the sand of ignorance, hoping death will be postponed or go away altogether, is wasteful insanity. Ignoring the subject can only harm us immeasurably when death's icy hand reaches out and grips us or one of our loved ones. The unshatterable fact is that, whether we like it or not, we all keep our appointment with death. Since it happens to all of us then, the big question is not "Will I die?" but "How shall I live until I die?"

The great theologian, Paul Tillich, questioned: "If one is not able to die, is he really able to live?" It is my hope that this book will help us all to be willing to accept the realities of facing death, and that there in our newfound willingness God will begin to shed a new light on our ability to go on, to persevere, to have hope, and even dream again, in spite of our terrible losses.

Those of us who are willing to take up the enormous task of communicating our fears or feelings; who discuss, even reluctantly, our wishes about death and dying; and who make the effort to allow God to work through the grief with us are the best equipped to live life to its fullest. Life, as Jesus intended, was meant to be lived abundantly. It was not to fill a cup halfway but to fill it past the brim and let it overflow.

Have you noticed that people who live realistic and truthful lives, who practice "the abundant life" the way the Bible teaches, seem to seize each experience, tragic or joyous, and squeeze every drop of learning out of it into their cup of life? Some of us are envious of the high quality of their lifestyle. But let's not forget what price that kind of honesty and courage exacts. Someone once wrote, "Some die without having really lived, while others continue to live in spite of the fact that they have died."

The psalmist David experienced living life in all its terrifying and joyous dimensions because he was well acquainted with grief, sorrow, and loss. I know this truth about him, else how could he have worked through these times of bereavement and still have penned these remarkable words? I believe David wrote because he had endured the slow burning fires of grief and knew what *living on* was all about. See his heart, and read of the lessons grief taught him:

> Lord, help me to realize how brief my time on earth will be. Help me to know that I am here for but a moment more. . . . We glide along the tides of time as swiftly as a racing river, and vanish as quickly as a dream. We are like grass that is green in the morning but mowed down and withered before the evening shadows fall. . . . Seventy years are given us! And some may even live to eighty. But even the best of these years are often emptiness and pain; soon they disappear, and we are gone. . . . Teach us to number our days and recognize how few they are; help us to spend them as we should.
>
> Psalm 39:4; 90:5–6, 10, 12

This book, then, is not really about death, but rather about living out our lives. It's about handling and coping with our days after a loved one has gone, about numbering and spending our time more insightfully and sensitively while we are here.

If we try to live this way, then when death does appear, we will be better prepared to meet it. We'll not spin a dark, opaque cocoon around our souls and miss death's meaningful stages or fear the way it brings so many shocking emotions.

We will know and recognize death. We will feel the raw pain of loss when our loved ones are gone. But we are not people without hope, and we need not try to stand on our own or work through our widely changing emotions and feelings alone. We have hope. We can trust in God's restorative powers.

When death comes not to someone else but to us, we can hold our heads high. We can understand, at least in part, that what is most important is not how or where we die, but *what we did with life* while we were here and able. These words were easy to write in 1974, but now it's 1993 and cancer has, perhaps, shortened my time. I wonder what I'll do with life while I'm still "here and able."

Oh, dear Lord, this book was painful to write because of all the remembering I had to do. Even now it hurts, but I want to write with an acutely sensitive pen, so don't spare memories for me.

I know *now* (hindsight is great) that you directed my way through my losses, but forgive me for thinking you had abandoned me. You were walking with me in the valley of the shadow of death, but my tears blinded me and my soul constricted within me. I marvel at your endless patience with me, Lord. Had I been you, I would have given up on me.

Thank you for leading me to the right books, both on the newsstand and, of course, in your Word. What you taught me through all of this has increased my capacity for life and enhanced the quality of my very existence. I'm glad—no, honored—that the way was so hard. It was the vehicle for you to use in my life in a meaningful, mighty way.

Lord, just a few weeks before she died, my mother gently wagged her finger at me and said "Honey, for thirty-four years I've taught you how a Christian should *live*. Now I'm going to show you how one *dies*." Remember?

Well, Lord, I pray you take those priceless lessons from the past and the now-lessons and mold them into this book.

Then perhaps, when we are to keep our appointments with death, we will have learned these incredibly difficult lessons so well, and lived so full a life for you, that we are able to say with David:

> But as for me, my contentment is not in wealth but in seeing you and knowing all is well between us. And when I awake in heaven, I will be fully satisfied, for I will see you face to face.
>
> Psalm 17:15

So, dear Savior,

> If I should die
> Before I wake,
> I pray thee, Lord,
> My soul to take.
>
> And as for those I love and leave behind
> Let them remember my last plea—
> I've gone home to God—I *am not dead*
> So let them sing no sad mourning songs for me.

2

Scared to Death of Dying

The fear of death is worse than death.
Robert Burton

After she transacted my banking business, the teller looked across the counter at me and said, "Okay, Joyce, tell me what you are writing now!"

"Well," I began, "actually I'm in between books at the moment. I'm finishing one and about to start another."

"The one you're going to start, what's it about?" she asked.

"It's a book on death," I started to explain, but she broke in and said, "That one, write it for me!"

"Why?" I asked.

"Oh, because I'm scared to death of dying." Her statement wasn't meant to be a play on words. She was quite serious.

"Do you mean you are afraid of the actual process of dying and how it will feel?" I asked, putting my own fear of the "process" into a question.

For a second or two she thought about it and then answered, "No, I guess I'm not so afraid of death for myself, but I do have this terrible fear about the possibility of my husband dying. What would I do? How would I survive? The whole thing really scares me."

Her terrible fear is familiar to all of us, although our fears of death strike us in different ways.

A child comes home from school to find his mother, brothers, and sisters gone and is gripped by the fear they have left him, or worse, that they have died and are never coming back again.

A bride begins to suffer from the same fear when her young husband has not returned home at his accustomed time.

A man driving along the freeway sees ahead of him an accident involving a car like the one his wife drives, and at the sight fear covers him with a wave of nausea and perspiration.

Parents hold tight to each other's hands as the doctor says, "I'm sorry, but the tests show your child has . . ." Fear plugs up their ears. They miss most of the diagnosis and have to call later to ask about what they didn't hear.

A teenager goes to the mortuary to pay his respects to a friend, but his fear of death is so strong that he leaves instantly and splatters his fear on the sidewalk outside.

A grandmother hides her fears during the day about her husband dying, but each night, even as she lies next to him, she dreams he has died. In her dreams, she endlessly drowns in a sea of fearful loneliness.

A man in the process of dying shares his greatest fear with his son when he says, "Teddy, boy, when I die, make sure I'm really dead before they put me in the ground. When I was little I was accidentally locked in a closet and the fear of being buried alive started there, so make sure I'm dead."

Young adults are haunted by a disturbing fear that the death of their parents will mean facing the end of family life as they know it, leaving them with insufficient wisdom to guide them into the future.

A doctor, in order to disguise his own fears about death, blurts out gruffly to a woman, "Your husband is dead," and abruptly turns on his heel and leaves her paralyzed in shock.

Another doctor, because he feels a patient's death means he has failed, makes it a policy never to be the one to level with a patient or tell loved ones that the patient has died. He denies death and its finality in another way by rarely, if ever, attending a funeral.

This terrible fear catches all of us. No matter how we look at it, even as mature, steady, reliable Christians, death is a very scary thing; if not scary, at least we'd really rather not deal with it, thank you very much. Our fears about death have often risen to the forefront of our minds, and they will probably continue to disturb us.

There is another aspect of our fear that concerns not death itself but the actual method of our dying. We wish death (*if* it should ever come to us) will arrive when we are eighty-five years old, after a nice, full life. We want the dying to come peacefully, preferably in our sleep. In the back of our minds lurks the dark thought that death may be quick and violent, or stripped of any dignity, or agonizingly drawn out with endless routines of pain and suffering. Most of us are not willing to face the fact that death may come in any one of these different ways. Certainly, they aren't the ways we hope to go.

In our minds we conjure up this peaceful deathbed scene. Here it is, the moment of death. The aged loved one sits up or opens his eyes and peacefully renders some beautiful last words of spiritual insight or a description of his first glimpse beyond heaven's gates. When death comes thus, we breathe a sigh of farewell; and we writers write about the poetic beauty of it all. But what of the time when death comes, and all dignity vanishes? We are quite reluctant to even think it may happen in this way.

When I asked the nurse how my mother died, she answered with a considerable amount of relief in her voice, "Oh, very quietly in her sleep." I've always wondered if that were true, or was the nurse shielding us both? Was the nurse just being kind by not telling me exactly how my mother died?

Knowing my outspoken mother, I tend to think she probably said with her last breath, "Oh, come on Lord, for goodness sake, hurry it up! Take me home!" But since I wasn't with her when she died, I don't know. It's a little fear that still nags at the back of my soul from time to time.

Joe Bayly, in telling of his five-year-old son's death from leukemia, related that his son died a violent death while hemorrhaging and screaming for a bedpan. For two years Joe was unable to speak of the manner of his son's death.

A chaplain I know told me that since he had been torpedoed and rescued at sea and had escaped death on several other occasions, he had discovered he was not afraid to die. He told me that his real concern at the time was whether or not he would die "like a man."

As I have already said, we want death to come to us when we are in our eighties, with dignity and preferably while we are sleeping.

I suspect my Aunt Grace was never able to put the memory of my grandmother's death to rest in her mind. It was in such dreadful contrast to my grandfather's quiet homegoing. My grandmother, in her eighties, a strong, marvelous Christian, died with no last words of comfort or wisdom. Even after a lifetime of goodness toward others and love of God, family, and her beloved America, she did not die peacefully or with dignity, although her soul beautifully belonged to God.

Grandma Uzon died as she was being held upright on the toilet, her bowels breaking and gushing from her. My aunt, holding her, had no way of holding back the contents of her own churning stomach. So my grandmother died with the unbelievable stench of broken bowels swirling below her and covered above with my aunt's irrestrainable vomit. It was a moment of unprecedented horror.

I doubt that my aunt was ever able to relate Grandma's death to the poetically beautiful verse in the Bible about how precious to God is the death of a saint. My grandmother, delightful child of God and yes, saint, did not die in an atmosphere that was ideally serene—it was hideous.

So we fear the method of dying as well as death itself. If it is not a conscious fear, it may well be a deeply submerged anxiety.

Since death happens only once to each of us, we are at as much of a loss to explain it as we are to explain our own birth. We cannot remember our time in our mothers' wombs before birth, nor can we remember anything about the process of being born. The events of our birth simply happened.

But the process of dying does worry us. How will we react? How will it be? When will it happen? One friend I know and love said, "Oh, Joyce, don't worry about dying. You'll make it! Everyone does, you know."

I suppose what we fear most about death are all the unanswered questions and the myriad mountains of unknowns. Most of us are not as outspoken about our fears as the teller in my bank. Still, death is a top fear in everyone's mind. The French philosopher Pascal noted that high priority when he remarked, "We spend our lives trying to take our minds off death."

I have been at a thousand funerals either as a mourner, a soloist, or both, but the idea that someday I or a member of my family will lie in a casket, surrounded by satin and flowers, is simply too incredible to take in. The very idea causes my fear to surge up and around me with such intensity that I force myself to escape mentally into more pleasant thoughts or memories of wonderful experiences.

How is it, as a Christian, that the fear of death can do this to me? I have reasoned with myself over this question and have thought, *I am confident about my position as a child of God. I have been a Christian for many years now and know full well where a Christian goes when he or she dies, so why does death (at least initially) terrify me?* Why is it every time I enter a hospital for any reason, I feel the fearful sting of death? The aroma of antiseptic solutions, the noise of clattering trays, and the attendants hurriedly rushing by pushing gurneys or carts, make me want to run out of there as fast as a scared jackrabbit in the middle of a busy highway.

"Men fear death because they refuse to understand it," said Cyrus L. Sulzberger in his book *My Brother Death*. So here's where we begin: with our fears. We start by trying to understand this mysterious process. We try with all our minds and souls to prepare ourselves for death's inevitable tap on the heartbeat of our existence.

During my process of trying to understand my fears, an incident happened in the foothills above my town in southern California. It shaved off a fair amount of fear from my soul, and I am indebted to Dr. Ted Cole for leading my mind through the maze of this lesson.

The local newspaper reported that a young boy had been bitten by a rattlesnake while he was hiking up one of the canyons in the foothills with his dad. The father had rushed his son to the nearest hospital, and after many hours of working on him the doctors had finally saved his life. It had been a very close call. At times the parents, even the doctors, had lost hope, but the boy had pulled through. The paper ran the story and printed a picture of the smiling little boy sitting up in bed with his relieved parents standing by.

Dr. Cole read the article in the pulpit the next Sunday. Then, to help us understand our fears of death, he asked us to imagine that after the boy's life was saved a man went back to the canyon, located the ledge where the boy had been climbing, and found the rattlesnake that had bitten him. He caught the snake, took it to a veterinarian, and had its venom completely removed, making the snake nonpoisonous. Then this man took the snake to the hospital to show the boy, explaining that this very rattlesnake, the one that had bitten him, was now harmless. The man then asked the boy if he wanted to hold the snake or even keep it as a pet.

At this point Dr. Cole questioned the congregation, "Do you think any amount of reasoning or explaining could get the boy to reach out and touch the snake, much less keep it?"

The answer from all of us was a resounding no! The boy would still be scared to death of that snake. There was no way he would be willing to accept this particular rattlesnake, or any other, because to him it would still look deadly. The snake wouldn't look one bit changed. No one would be able to convince the boy it was harmless. His terrified screams would have echoed throughout the hospital.

Here, then, is part of the answer to why death frightens us so much. While as Christians we know Christ has removed the sting of death and death can never kill us for eternity—*death still exists.* It is still fearfully ugly and repulsive. We probably will never be able to regard, imagine, or fantasize death as being a loving friend. Whenever and wherever death connects with us, no matter how strong we are in our Christianity or how well we are prepared for it, it still slides and slithers into our lives and freezes us with fear. Such is the nature of death.

With a touch of fear in her voice, my mother, a few years before her death, talked briefly about her own dying. I was at her house helping her clean out a long-neglected linen closet. She'd been a little less noisy than usual; in fact, she was so pensive that I finally said, "Penny for your thoughts, Mother."

She looked down, straightened some bath towels in her arms, and without looking up said, "Well, I'm not trying to be morbid, but lately I've had this feeling that I'll not live too many years longer. I feel I'll never see Marilyn or Cliff grown or married. In fact, I don't think God is going to grant me the normal life span of seventy-five-years."

A small chill ran down my back. She had voiced what most of us think once in a while about our own dying. Occasionally, during a trying time when we are in a depressed mood, we all fantasize about how it would be to die young or suddenly or right now, and we spend a brief time on the "what

ifs" of our own dying. I was tempted to brush Mother's remark away, pat her on her head, and say something smart
and completely untrue like, "Honey, you're too mean to die."
But the fear that it just might be true hovered in the hallway
like a faded fragrance from an old spice bouquet hidden
among the linens, and I couldn't be smart or funny about it.
She had a gift of discernment about other people, so why not
about herself?

The phone rang and ended our conversation. After that,
time diverted it into a new direction. Neither of us brought
up her feeling about dying again. Since then I've wondered
about that day and pondered, if the phone had not rung when
it did would she have gone on and told me her terrible secret?
It was a secret that must have lent authenticity that day to
her feelings of dying. But I'll never know.

She alone had access to the information about some lumps
in her breast, and she kept it from us. Years before our day
by the linen closet, she had discovered the small lumps in
her left breast. Her fears about the unutterable word *cancer*
made her lock up the secret in her heart and deliberately
throw away the key. She was like many others of her generation. If a woman even suspected breast cancer, she would
believe it meant surgery (or cutting, as Mother would have
called it) and would quietly sentence herself to death. She
would seek no medical help, believing all the doctors wanted
to do was "cut into her." Tragically, her silence would hurry
death along for sure. Many of this generation and a good
many women in my generation died early in life because they
did not seek help soon enough. Many, like my mother, would
later die saying to their daughters, "Joyce, don't you *dare*
do what I did. Promise me you'll go to your doctor for regular checkups."

Since she was an avid reader, I wondered how in the world
Mother had missed those magazine articles on cancer, and
particularly breast cancer, that were just beginning to show
up in print. I had no way of knowing that because she knew

she had lumps she'd studiously avoided reading anything with the word *cancer* in it.

There was another reason for locking up her secret, and it had to do with her strong faith in God. She was on completely familiar terms with almighty God. She had watched him all through her life directing her path. He had rescued, healed, and comforted her each year of her life that she had served him. "He'll take care of those lumps," was her reasoning. So, in childlike faith, she gave him her dreadful secret and left it with him. It was God's problem, not hers, and God would handle it. I'm sure she never intended for any of us to ever know, so she never told us about the lumps, only about the feeling she'd die early.

Some might say it was by accident that we found out later, but I think not. God surprised us by giving her secret away for her. It was a few years after we'd cleaned out the linen closet when one day she turned the corner in the hall, misjudged the position of the kitchen doorway, and ran smack into it. Later that night she was undressing just as my father came into the bedroom. It took no more than a second's glance at the ugly bruise and swelling on Mother's breast before he decided he would take her to the doctor first thing the next morning. Meekly she agreed.

The next day, my father phoned me and told me of Mother's bruise and her visit to the doctor. It had taken the doctor only a brief examination to discover large groupings of lumps. It took no time at all to put her into the hospital and schedule a radical mastectomy for the following day. Her secret was out.

As I drove to the hospital the next afternoon, I remembered our conversation about her not living a full life. She was fifty-four years old. Words like *tumor, cancer,* and *biopsy* all floated in and out of my mind that day. I was very frightened and began the first serious thinking about her death.

It seems to me that death never hits us all at once but rather in surges like the waves of the sea. Some waves cause little

more than ripples, and then the sea becomes still; others begin
building, and one by one they get larger. Sometime around
the seventh or eighth wave it builds up its enormous strength
and hits the beach with unleashed force.

Death comes like those waves, and daily we lose a little
more ground. Our old tissue dies and drops and the new
develops, only to complete the circle and die. Paul, in the
New Testament, said we die daily. *How true,* I thought as I
drove. *But not yet. Please God, not yet.*

When I reached Mother's room, she was sleeping lightly.
I touched her face. She opened her eyes, recognized me,
started to smile, and then grew terribly serious as she remembered something disturbing. She reached for my hand and
said, "Joyce-Honey, they took it. It's gone. I have no . . ."
Her voice trailed off as she couldn't say the word *breast.*

Even though my generation is far better read and open
than hers about the care and treatment of breast cancer, I
still remember the words *radical mastectomy* clobbering the
breath right out of my lungs. The small box of fear inside me
was rapidly expanding, and I took on a whole shipment of
anxiety.

Mother was explaining to me what had transpired, and
her tone of voice was the most bewildered I'd ever heard.
"When I came in yesterday"—she shook her head in disbelief—"I signed some papers . . . I didn't read too much of
them because the words were very medical-sounding. I
didn't know I was giving them permission to take my . . . I
was drowsy with some shot . . . I didn't know, Joyce." Then,
with her brown eyes intently looking into mine, she finished,
"They amputated *me* . . . they took my, they took *me* . . .
it's gone."

"Mother, why didn't you tell anyone about the lumps
when you first found them? Why didn't I know?" I whispered
as gently as I could.

"Oh, honey, I just thought . . . oh, you know . . . the Lord
has always taken care of every need . . . I didn't want to bother

you about it," she explained. She was still too stunned to figure it out or go on.

I left her bed later and went out to find her doctor. He
saw me coming down the hall, stuck out his hand, grabbed
mine, and said, "I'm pretty sure we got it all." Those words
washed another surge of fear over my soul. I managed to
form a one-word question, "Malignant?"

"Yes."

A friend of mine wrote, "Normally we think of fear as a
negative force in our lives; however, it can and does perform
at least one positive function for us—it wakes us up! Not
many people fall asleep when the adrenaline is flowing." So
it was for me. That day well marked the beginning of a big
adrenaline flow in my life; and after that, falling asleep at night
became a difficult task.

That big, new, ugly fear caused me to look long and seriously at my mother. I was filled with a desire to know all
about her in every dimension. I also took a good, long look
at my own feelings and fears about the subject of death and
about my own (sometime in the future) death. I noticed that
while the fire of fear certainly still burned, it seemed to be
contained and confined a bit.

I began to feel a compelling urgency about my own life
and the time allotted to me. What was I doing with my years?
How was I spending my life's energies? What if I had ten
days, thirty years, or that highly prized life span of seventy-
five years to live? Was I eagerly participating in the celebra-
tion of life, or was I plodding dully along from one rut to
another?

I decided I would relearn all the things my mother had
taught me about observing everybody and everything that
went on around me. I'd train myself in earnest to see all I
could see, hear all I could hear, and be all I could be for however many years I had. It was, has been, and is an exhausting
decision—but worth it. I am grateful to God for the lessons
the fear of death has taught me.

I hate the method God used, taking a child and grandfather and finally my mother, but experiencing those losses
rearranged many of my life's priorities and goals. Today, since
cancer has invaded me, I'm once again reexamining those
priorities and goals. My daughter, Laurie, and my sister, Marilyn, are also in the process of dealing with their own priorities and goals. It is an exhausting task.

Back in the '60s I began to consider death and dying in very
personal terms. I realized that my attitude, my ability to cope,
and my acceptance of my own eventual death would depend
heavily on how I had faced or avoided death in general.

I now know the fear of death is a universal human trait
built into all of us. I must not be shocked or surprised by it
in my own life. I must not be hard or judgmental toward others when I see it in theirs. I must be willing to admit that
dying is not always well preceded by notice. It can be shockingly instantaneous and completely without any redeeming
grace or peace.

A seventeen-year-old boy like Mike falls asleep at the wheel
of his car, hits a tree, and is instantly incinerated. A girl like
Debbie is kidnapped, raped, and murdered within a span of
five torturous hours. A grandmother like mine dies amid un-
dignified chaos. These are the methods death sometimes uses.

We must all hold high in our hearts the moving truth that
all of these who died as Christians in such sudden and horrid vulgarity have reached their ultimate destination of
heaven. They are with God. In spite of the transportation
used and the unacceptable method of traveling, they have
completed their trip and have arrived. They are now gloriously alive! This truth gives us one small, soft pocket for our
grief, but the pain is not eased much. If we are willing to lay
our fears out on the table and acknowledge their presence,
however, we're halfway home to mastering a degree of acceptance of them. We can even begin to see a little hope out
there, and a healing takes place within us.

Yet because the fear of death and dying is never fully con-

querable in us, I am like the little boy recovering from his snakebite. I am unable to pet the rattlesnake.

My mother was released from the hospital after her mastectomy and came home in what could only be described as high, joyous spirits. It was as if she'd deliberately neglected to pack her fears or her disappointments in her little suitcase. I was baffled by her change of emotions. She treated her surgery with the same importance one gives an uncomplicated tonsillectomy done in a doctor's office under a local anesthetic.

Even the first weeks after her surgery, the only plans she had were to recover. I was pleased about this mentally healthy attitude of hers. But she puzzled me again and again as she would not let me mention or question anything about her surgery, her illness, or especially the word *cancer*. Once when I tried she quickly shushed me up with, "Now, now, the doctors got 'it' all." She followed that with, "And now I'm going to get well."

She had never been of the Christian Science persuasion, but at one point I told her she'd make a great one! She just laughed and told me (again) I was taking her surgery too seriously. God had taken care of her as he promised and now there was nothing more to worry about. "The battle's over and won!" she said victoriously.

I believe now that Mother took a line from one of her favorite devotional books, *Streams in the Desert,* and made it into a banner of truth inside her heart. The line from the poem reads ". . . while God's assuring voice sings love across the storm." Mother would hear only God's song as she endured the storm, and she was beautifully peaceful.

Or perhaps it was another favorite, a chapter in the Book of Psalms, which gave her a sense of everything's going to be all right. She knew these words by heart:

> My voice shalt thou hear in the morning, O Lord; in the morning will I direct my prayer unto thee, and will look up.
>
> Psalm 5:3 KJV

Since I knew nothing at the time of the ways of grief-losses, I didn't realize until many months later that Mother had also done something else: She had gone into the closet of complete denial and had firmly shut the door behind her.

3
Oh, God—No!

You can't heal a wound by saying it's not there!
Jeremiah 6:14

A car carrying six teenagers to a football game swerved at high speed and crashed into a concrete wall. The driver of the car was a sixteen-year-old girl. As they all lay trapped inside, she listened to the sounds of dying coming from her five friends. This lone survivor recalled that one thing each of her friends uttered before he or she died was, "Oh, God—no!"

Whether it is the knowledge of our own imminent death or the news of someone else's death, the reaction seems to be the same. It does not matter if it is a sudden death like that of the teenagers in this tragic accident or a death painfully endured and prolonged for years. The actual moment of death is always too much to understand. Our knowledge of a death brings an immediate crisis to our lives, and part (perhaps a larger part than we realize) of our crisis centers on denial. Denial becomes one of the parts of our mourning song that is the most difficult to understand.

The second we are told of someone's death we cannot believe it. Our emotions gather forces within us and shout, "No! This can't be true!"

An older woman, on learning her husband of fifty-six years had died suddenly while she was outside gardening, looks incredulously at her granddaughter and says, "Oh, no, that's simply not true. Why, he wouldn't do that without me. We were supposed to go together."

Denial comes easily to us, for it's too difficult to comprehend never seeing that person here on earth again. It's unthinkable to imagine the silence of never hearing that one's voice again. It's impossible to fathom living each day without that one!

When my husband leaned over my bed as I lay in the hospital and said, "Hon, it's all over, David is with the Lord," my first cry was, "Oh, no." Months before, my doctors had suggested I prepare myself because my baby, with an Rh-negative blood factor, might not survive birth. But even with more preparation—and I did prepare—I wonder if I would ever have been ready for his death. I doubt it.

On hearing of our loved ones' deaths, our thoughts may be stunned or blurred; but one thing we know for sure: They are not gone. It is not true. Oh, how we cling to the hope that nothing we are hearing is true. If you told me this second that my husband, one of my children or grandchildren, or any loved one had been diagnosed with a terminal illness or had died the hour before, I would react with the same, "Oh, no" with which I responded to David's death.

I have always talked freely with my entire family about death and dying. I suppose if any family has communicated, discussed, and faced death it is mine; but still, when the knowledge of a death comes, it is impossibly heavy. I know now that even with preparation, denial swells like an ugly bruise immediately after death's overwhelming blow. While we can prepare ourselves for death up to a point, we are rarely able to adjust to it with calm and instant acceptance.

A man recalled the moments of denial he had when he heard the doctor diagnose his life-threatening disease. "The doctor's words hit me with the sting of dynamite," he said. He described denial symptoms as burning sensations in his chest, pounding in his head, numbness in his arms and legs, and feet that had "gone all rubbery" under him. Denial not only hits us mentally with "Oh, no"; it affects us physically as well.

Before writing this book, I had a long interview with my longtime friend, the brilliant and sensitive surgeon Dr. James White. I wondered with Jim about the whys of death denial, and we talked about some of his terminally ill patients. Since I knew Jim understood the emotional problems and complex crises that death-knowledge produces in patients and their families, I asked, "Do you always come straight out and level with a patient and his family about death?"

His answer came slowly and thoughtfully, "Yes, about 99 percent of the time." Then he added, "But I definitely postpone the news if it in any way jeopardizes the patient's well-being." He said he did not tell patients of their true condition if they were in danger of cardiac arrest because that news might bring on the fatal attack. Also, he did not tell the news to a patient immediately out of surgery or one day out of intensive care while the patient was still in critical condition; and if a patient right out of surgery asked a direct question about dying, he would buy time (usually a day or two) by saying he was "waiting for test results." He did this for patients only when he felt the knowledge of their exact condition would be detrimental to their general health. It's possible that there are many other ways of handling grief-knowledge, but I believe Dr. White's approach is medically sound and emotionally right.

But most of Dr. White's patients were kindly and gently told the truth. My talk with Jim that night confirmed for me that I would want a doctor to treat me exactly as Jim treats his patients. I would want, if it were at all possible, to know the extent of damages and the professional opinion of my doctor, even if it meant his telling me I was facing death.

I said to my oncologist just recently, "I know, Doctor, you have patients who do not wish to know anything about this illness, but not me. I'm a writer and I want to know the worst-case scenario and the best-case scenario about my cancer so I can deal with it on my own terms."

Perhaps you are a person who does not want to know the worst-case/best-case prognoses, and there is nothing wrong with that. Knowing or not knowing becomes a personal choice for each of us. I remember a family who did not know the father was dying of cancer until his last three months. He finally called them together and told them the nature and seriousness of his illness. As his condition worsened, he and his family said their good-byes and were able to talk freely of his death. His family was all with him when he died.

During the reading of his will, the lawyer gave the widow and her children a box of tapes the father had made eight or nine months before he died, right after his doctor had told him his condition was terminal. In those tapes his children heard their father's special words for each of their upcoming birthdays through the teens to their twenty-first year. To his wife he left a number of tapes to help her adjust to everything from check writing to caring for the house, and he also expressed his loving wishes that she marry again. He made tapes that were special messages for his family's first Christmas without him and even a tape for his first grandchild, whenever that child was born.

He was able to leave his family these treasured tapes because a wise doctor told him the worst scenario of his illness and he accepted that he was dying. Recording those tapes was probably the hardest thing he ever did. But he had worked through his denial, and his wife and family were sustained for years by the legacy he so lovingly left. I am now in the process of recording my own tapes.

Dr. White is one of those gifted men who can give such

news in the best possible way. I asked him if he had a formula for divulging this information. I particularly wanted to know what he would tell young doctors about breaking this kind of news to patients. He told me the main lesson he would teach young doctors about working with the dying would focus on these four words: *gradual with the information.* He said, however, when death was not drawn out but came unexpectedly, the "gradual information" would be handled differently.

For the slowly dying patient, a wise doctor will carefully watch the patient's responses and reactions and give out information as the patient is able to take it in. If the patient asks a direct question, the caring doctor will give a direct answer. It is important for doctors not to lie to their patients at any time. Dr. White said he did not lie, even by implication. He felt it was absolutely imperative to establish an honest level of communication between patient and doctor.

"Very often," he continued, "a patient will ask, 'Is it a tumor?' I'll answer, 'Yes,' Then a day, maybe two days later, the same patient will look up at me and ask, 'Malignant?' I'll say, 'Yes,' and depending on the patient's responses after that, I will talk with him as long or as little as he wants."

A wise doctor, in giving gradual yet honest information, is giving the patient's right to denial a chance to work itself out. Jim's sensitivity to the patient's questions, his alertness to their specific needs, and his views on helping patients and families accept death made me more and more aware of the Christlike, loving concern hovering over this man like a heavenly mantle. My friend Dr. White had no training in death seminars, but his honesty and his own acceptance of death allow him to help people.

Doctors have always been more than willing to teach us the entire birth process with printed information, long talks, or even classes. In 1952 I took six weeks of classes from my doctor's staff when I was pregnant with my first child. I was so well prepared for that birth I even had a checklist of the hospital routine in my hand when I entered the labor room.

The nurse in charge came in, talked with me a few minutes while I was in labor, and asked me how many children I had. When I told her I was having my first, she said, "Oh, then you have got to be Dr. Cartwright's patient, right?"

"Yes," I replied. "How did you know?"

"All his patients are so well prepared to give birth that they come in with very few questions, are familiar with hospital procedure, and fully accept the birth process."

But it was vastly different for the dying process. When I first wrote this book in 1973 I was aware of the hospice organization in England, but I knew of no such services or classes which were set up in hospitals or doctors' offices to help the dying or the families of the dying cope with the death process going on around them. It seemed to me the need for such classes was shockingly enormous. What I'm suggesting here is a pre-death support group. Of course, we need support groups after a loved one's death, but for the terminally ill and the family around the bed the need is even more urgent.

Judging from what I have read and heard, a high percentage of doctors need some concrete advice on how to communicate with a patient about his or her terminal illness. For many years there were no classes on death and dying offered even to medical students who expected to deal with dying in their practice. To be so feeble in our attempts to educate and equip medical professionals and clergy for the titanic task of helping others face and accept death says a great deal about our society's frantic denial of death. At least now there are well-established hospice services and a growing number of classes and seminars available to help doctors understand death and how to treat the terminally ill.

Twenty or thirty years ago the doctor's work was over once a patient had died. The idea that the bereaved family desperately needed the doctor's healing services did not occur to him, or if it did, he did not see it as his responsibility. But if doctors, nurses, or clergy do not give help to the dying and their families, who will?

Some doctors have allowed their own fears of death to rob them of all sensitivity. They develop a steel-like shield of brusqueness. They have their own agenda for a patient's treatment; then if the patient dies, they abruptly announce, "He's gone" or "It's over," and instantly beat a retreat from the room to avoid any emotional outburst from the family. Precisely at the moment when a family has many anxiety-filled questions for which they desperately need answers, the doctor leaves. Or the nurse who has been so attentive and active around the patient suddenly clams up and claims instant ignorance. Fear and denial often bring about scenes like these.

Still other doctors rationalize that most dying patients do not want the truth so they should not be given the knowledge of the seriousness of their illness. "No good will come from it," they say. Or if a patient's family tells the doctor, "Don't tell Aunt Ida she's dying; she won't be able to take it," he helps their (and his own) denial by respecting their wishes. It is my personal belief that this type of thinking and judgment will seriously jeopardize that family's chances of moving into acceptance of death later on. Doctor Kübler-Ross feels the question should not be "Should we tell?" but "How do I share this with my patient?"

I will always be grateful for my surgeon, Dr. Patricia Morrison, who was the first to tell me I had cancer. It was while I was in the recovery room after the biopsy had been performed. She had told me before the surgery that I would have an answer before I left the hospital that day as to what kind of lumps I had. After surgery, I opened my eyes, saw Francis, my husband, at the end of my bed, and then looked into the face of my surgeon.

Loudly, so I could hear, she said, carefully enunciating the words, "Joyce, you have cancer. . . . There are two kinds of breast cancer. . . . Unfortunately, you have a mix of both." All of us in that room, including the two nurses, were very still; then, in that quietness, I heard Dr. Morrison say softly, "I'm so sorry."

I want a doctor who has Dr. Morrison's and Dr. White's blend of professional medical counsel and clear communication that is both gentle and sensitive to me as a person. When we do have doctors like these two, our run toward denial is not so swift. We are helped immeasurably to begin coping with our devastating knowledge.

Dr. White told me that a final goal in his formula for helping a person through the death-knowledge crisis was always to hold out a glimmer of hope to the patient. No matter how slight the hope, how farfetched or illusive, he felt it was absolutely necessary to talk of hope. Maintaining his honesty, he would give no false hopes, but he would find some ray of hope to leave with his patient.

Stewart Alsop, a man dying of leukemia, wrote in his excellent book *Stay of Execution:* "A man who must die, will die more easily if he is left a little spark of hope that he may not die after all. My rule would be: Never tell a victim of terminal cancer the whole truth—tell him that he *may* die, even that he will *probably* die, but do not tell him that he *will* die."

Nobody, not even the most brilliant of our professional medical scientists, knows exactly when or in what way death will come. They can give educated, medically wise judgments, but death has its own way of surprising us by doing the unexpected. "Some patients," Dr. White said, "give all the various signs and signals of not lasting the night, yet the next morning's dawn finds them having passed the death crisis and well established into recovery. Still other patients slip away right before our astonished eyes. We are stunned and can only say, 'How did it happen?'" Another doctor said disbelievingly, "I was standing right next to her, and I never even saw it coming!"

Not knowing how much time one has is particularly true if one has cancer, because no one knows exactly what makes latent cancer cells begin to divide from healthy cells and multiply. No one knows what the cure is, and there are hundreds of different kinds of cancer. It's no wonder the easiest and least confusing path to take is denial. Much is unexplainable about death, hence our fearful thoughts and our death-denial rituals.

Many ministers are guilty of death denial, though they play it out a little differently than do doctors. The minister occupies himself with "being there." He changes hats and suddenly becomes a highly trained nurse's aide, getting right to his busy work of shaving the patient or straightening out the tray on the nightstand. If the patient or the family really get down to talking about death, the minister swiftly retreats by reading a well-quoted psalm or ends all discussion by saying, "Let's have a word of prayer." His problems with death rob the dying person and the family of the best tool they could have in coping with death: discussing their fears with someone they trust.

I'll always be grateful to one minister who I believe had properly accepted death. He was Reverend Warner, a fantastic saint of God in his seventies. Everyone, young and old, called him Pop Warner. January 1, 1965, the morning after my son David had died, Pop stole quietly into my room. He touched my arm, and I woke to see him standing over me.

"I know about your baby," he said, not wasting any time by ignoring the fact that David had died, which helped me to stay out of denial.

"I'm glad to see you, Pop. Please sit down," I urged.

"No, my dear, if I sit down I'll stay too long, and it will tire you, so I'll stand. Now, tell me, how is this going for you?"

Then that dear man stood and listened as I poured out my anguished heart. I told him I was not handling this well *at all*, and I told him the staff hadn't allowed me to hold David. He did not lecture me or offer any advice or words, although he was more than capable. He didn't busy himself with taking out the wilted flowers beside my bed. He just listened. Listening—the greatest gift one person can give to another. He looked me directly in the eye as I told him how badly it was going for me. When I'd finally said everything I so desperately needed to say, he bent over my bed and prayed, "Oh Lord, you are here and you've heard all that Joyce has said. Now you know the way to heal her heart. Heal her quickly, Lord; bind up her wounds; we need her." And then, knowing it was hard for me to believe David was really dead, he gently helped me take my first tottering steps away from denial toward acceptance by adding, "And, dear Lord, take loving care of that precious baby for Joyce."

An hour or so after he'd gone, I saw the little book he had left on my nightstand without telling me. Over and over in the following days I read and reread the Bible verses in that little book. The precious words and the memory of Pop Warner helped ease me out of denial into acceptance.

I thank God for ministers like Pop, who never once evaded or ignored my need to talk about my son's death; who didn't pat me on the back, telling me "Everything is going to be all right" but patiently let me explain why I thought everything was all wrong. I thank God for doctors like Dr. White who take time to help heal the wrenching pain of the bereaved loved ones who must go on living after the patient has gone. I thank God, too, for the new breed of doctors like Dr. Elisabeth Kübler-Ross, who emerged in the mid-'60s, to take on the monumental task of breaking down the walls of our last great taboo: the dying process. I am hopeful now, for we are seeing a few courageous men and women who are stepping forth to say, "Hey, let's not run and hide from this, and let's not morbidly take death to our arms as a lover, but let's learn what we can from the dying and from each other about the death crisis!"

I'm also grateful to God for the growing number of medical professionals, clergy, social workers, and counselors who are willing to help separate fact from fantasy and who are also willing to help people articulate their feelings about death. As I said previously, we all have the general, vague feeling we will die sometime, but most of us deny it by saying *but not yet!* Most experts think the more we have expressed our feelings and fears to someone else, the more adept we will be in handling death when it does come our way. There seem to be fewer surprises and fewer problems if death has not been completely blocked out of our conversations or shoved under the rug.

Stephanie, a beautiful young woman, sat in my living room for a number of hours and told me how death had touched her. Just a bare two weeks before, she and her husband John had been climbing up a small canyon to cut down their first Christmas tree. Suddenly John experienced some intense chest pains, and a little more than twenty-four hours later this young, vibrant, twenty-six-year-old man was dead.

As she sat on my couch, Stephanie shed some tears and choked back some others, but on the whole she was poised and more than willing to share her innermost self. I questioned her about denial, wondering how John's death had become real to her. She answered that they had prepared themselves.

Theirs was a marriage with all channels of communication wide open. They loved each other and God. Both had discussed their thoughts, dreams, ideas, and wishes. Both had given their lives for as much time as they had to being God's people. They had talked of death as routinely as they had talked of every subject under the sun. When death came, it was horrible but perhaps not as devastating as it could have been. She knew John's wishes. At one point, however, she dropped her God-given acceptance and went back to denial saying, "I can't believe it's happened."

I thought as I watched her that day, shaking her head in disbelief for just a second, that I wished I could be with her two months later rather than now in these first two weeks.

If we are Christians we experience a remarkable thing. Very often from the moment of someone's death, as it was in Stephanie's experience, we are surrounded, cushioned, and protected by God's beautiful cocoon of peace. We make a hundred difficult decisions and feel buoyed and spiritually uplifted. We go to the funeral with hope, glorious hope, pervading our hearts and minds. But about two months later, when Christian friends have gone back to their work and have eased up on their prayers for us, our world falls apart.

A widow who "did so well" at the funeral can't figure out how to balance the checkbook two months later, and the tears of frustration cover her stack of checks and financial papers.

A mother who held all the family together when their daughter died falls apart three months later as she passes her daughter's old room.

A man who shed no tears at his wife's funeral is driving to work and, hearing his wife's favorite song on the car radio, has to pull off the road because his sobbing is uncontrollable.

Just a few months after a funeral, we all begin to wonder why we were so calm at the funeral, and why now, much later, we can't seem to pull anything together. We feel like we are actually falling apart all over again, like death just happened, and it doesn't make any sense. How could we go through a funeral with our heads held high in complete acceptance and two months later be back in denial again? God was so real, so present, so comforting at first—now he seems to be gone.

About then some wise-enough-to-know-better Christian is shocked by a widow's actions and questions, "Why, my goodness, what's happened to Mrs. So-and-So? She took her husband's death in stride at the funeral. Now look at her. I wish she'd snap out of this and be her normal self again. Too bad, though; I thought she was such a strong Christian. What's happened to her faith?"

Often we mistake the numbing effects of shock for "in stride." Because we took the funeral in stride, we're fine—not so. Mental and emotional shock is the body's protection, and God allows us to be gently covered by it at the moments surrounding death.

Actually, at the funeral we are experiencing the normal workings and pattern of denial and acceptance. God beautifully shields us at first to get us through; then, as the realities of death settle in, so does our grief. It is normal to pull one's self together for the funeral, and it is also completely normal to fall apart in the days, weeks, months, and even years to come.

As I talked with Stephanie that day I plainly saw and heard all about the unique way God eases us through the initially hard, brutal part of death. But I knew her time for waking to the reality of John's death and learning to live in a world without John would come later. It would be strange if it didn't. The death knowledge would hit, and it would have little to do with her lack of faith or trust in the Lord.

Two months after I visited with Stephanie, a friend of hers asked me to remember Stephanie in prayer. When I asked why, her friend said, "It's really strange. You know she seemed to take John's death so well, but now . . . now it's really hit her, and she's really having a rough time."

I am confident that Stephanie worked through this in the following months, for she had a very willing desire to let God work out the grief in her life. I know he did, but it probably was not done overnight. For several years she needed the loving prayers of family and friends just as much, if not more, than when John died.

It's hard to grasp and understand the workings of denial, either the immediate "Oh, no" or the prolonged after-death kind, but I think how we cope with denial may be predetermined by our childhood experiences. I remember my father telling me about his own father's death. He spoke of it a few months after my mother had died, and I wished I'd known it earlier. Perhaps I would have understood many things relating to my father and his denial.

My dad was about eight years old when his schoolteacher told him his aunt had come to take him home. Without a word, his aunt met him in the hall and hurriedly hustled him outside. He recalled vividly the ride home in the horse-drawn wagon.

As they rode, my dad asked, "Why did I have to leave school, Auntie?"

With no show of emotion, either facial or verbal, his aunt abruptly stated, "Your father is dead." No explanation, no kind words, no empathy or sympathy followed. They rode all the way to his house in stony silence. As the weight of her words began to crush him, the tears started pouring down his face.

His aunt, seeing his tears, instantly slapped his face and yelled, "Stop that crying right now! Don't you *dare* cry."

Those moments, so long past, were the moments when Dad first shut off his feelings and emotions, and that closed door would be shut all his life. His family's attitude toward death carried over into my life. When I was growing up, I could never understand why Dad got so upset whenever I cried. He'd tell me, "Stop right now!" Later he'd tell others, "Joyce flushes easily" to explain my tears. He *forbade* me to cry. For years he made crying something only a very weak person would indulge in. Not until Dad told me about his father's death and that dreadful scene with his aunt did I begin to see where his attitude toward my tears, and later his death denial, had started.

His experience and story, even though I heard it after my mother's death, answered a number of my questions. Had I known of Dad's background, I could have used that knowledge to good advantage. Certainly, I would have been much more tolerant of Dad's denial and his refusal to believe death would take my mother.

I wish I could have read Dr. Kübler-Ross's book, particularly the chapter on denial, before my mother's illness. It would have given me a lot of insight about my parents' denial of death. I would have been better equipped to develop a patient, understanding attitude toward them, and I probably wouldn't have reacted in anger toward my father and sister when I tried to cope with the difficult aspects of their denial. I could have given them grace as they denied Mother's illness and subsequent death. I could have helped them move through denial more smoothly into at least a partial acceptance.

Is all denial bad? I certainly thought so. I was one for facing the truth, no matter how painful. Somewhere along the line, maybe after years of trying to hold back or stop my tears, I felt that denial, like tears, was a weak or stupid trait. I wish I'd known it's a vitally normal emotion that desperately needs to be voiced. I was proud of, and self-righteous about, my ability to face things head-on. Such thinking set me up well for falling hard later on.

I now know that denial is needed to act as an emotional buffer or safety zone after we see the reality of someone else's death or our own imminent death. It gives our ravaged souls a time to draw back and rest a bit. It gives a temporary measure of healing. It can be used in our lives as a God-given diversion.

We have a caring responsibility to the dying and to the bereaved even when we ourselves are part of the grieving family. One of the regrets of my life is that during my mother's illness I was not as sympathetic with my family as I should have been. I was quite unprepared and unwilling to witness denial in a mother who had always met life's problems head-on. It didn't dawn on me that denial would hit her, come on strong, then fade, then attack again. It simply never occurred to me that my father's bizarre actions, like buying my mother a four-hundred-dollar refrigerator just weeks before she died, were caused by his patterns of denial. I had much to learn.

One year after her surgery my mother experienced every evidence of complete denial, and without words, friction ran high between us. We had never discussed the possibilities of tumors in the other breast or the possible need for a second mastectomy. Her doctors at UCLA Medical Center wanted her to begin radiation treatments (or cobalt treatments, as they were then called), and still we did not talk about the dark shadow we both saw. We certainly never said the word *cancer* out loud. Mother was only able to say *cancer* if she was talking about someone else's cancer. When she talked to my sister, Marilyn, Mother would pat her chest and call it "this sickness." I grew quite impatient and intolerant with her attitude. I was one indignant daughter.

When Christmas rolled around, I was eager to set her straight about her blatant denial. It was my feeling that she should face up to the fact that she was showing evidence of advanced breast cancer. In a great burst of sincere stupidity, I wrote on the back of my Christmas card to her:

> Dearest Mother,
>
> Knowing full well that this may be our last Christmas together, I still feel it will be the sweetest yet. Who can tell just which of us will not be here next year—yet to us our joy in Christ will overtake any sorrow.
>
> "When thou passeth through the waters, I will be with thee and through the rivers, they shall not overflow thee."
>
> Joyce

(Actually, it did turn out to be her last Christmas.)

Little did I dream, in my arrogant burst of let-me-set-you-straight superiority, that she would react to it exactly as if she had just run barefoot over several hundred sharp tacks. She flew at me from every direction—by phone, by letters, and in person! She was mad as a wet hen at my insinuating that she might not be well or that she was anything but extremely healthy. I could scarcely have foreseen that my words would cause such an emotional fury—but they did! Over and over again she hotly denied she was sick.

I believe it was Sigmund Freud who thought most people want to avoid death so much that they develop a basic dishonesty toward it. Seeing my ultrahonest and direct mother developing this type of dishonesty was unthinkable to me! I know now that when people are in denial, there is very little anyone else can do to pull them out of it.

The culmination of this time of denial in her life came when she received a letter from her dear friend Dale Evans Rogers. Dale's accomplishments in show business were well known to everyone; but to my mother, Dale was simply her dearest friend. My mother was the spiritual counselor for Dale's Christian sorority in the San Fernando Valley. They saw each other quite often, but during the time of my mother's illness Dale had been out of town on her usual hectic schedule. Someone had finally told her of my mother's surgery and of the malignant tumors.

Dale, absolutely no stranger to death, having lost her daughters Robin and Debbie, wrote my mother a letter right out of her heart. She said she'd just learned of my mother having cancer. (Whoops! Big mistake!) Then she talked about how wonderful it would be for Mother to soon be in heaven with our Lord. (I can just see Mother's reaction as she read *that* line.) Then Dale, because her own acceptance of death was so real, alive, and well adjusted, said she wished she could go to heaven with Mother. Dale told of her children already with the Lord and how she longed to see them. She ended by writing in her own poetic style that she wished Mother could take her with her when she went. I thought it was the most meaningful and beautiful letter I'd ever read in my life. My mother's reaction was just the opposite. She was furious.

It was one of the few times that something about death was funny. There my mother lay in bed, too sick to be up and about, with my letter and Dale's in her hand. She was bawling me out for even thinking such thoughts. Her deep brown-black eyes were just snapping as she scolded me, and I remember thinking, *For one who is so sick Mother's got a lot of fight left in her.* I never loved her more, but I was of no help to her whatsoever! I knew so little about the ways of denial.

I wish I'd known denial is usually a temporary state of mind. At least I wish I'd known that it tends to come and go once it starts in the terminally ill person. During the next few months Mother laid her denial aside only briefly and in rare moments, such as if she felt very sick. But as soon as she would begin to feel better, her confidence of recovery would increase, and she would resume her original denial premise.

Much later, when she was not responding to the 5-FU (fluorouracil) of chemotherapy or the cobalt treatments and had found that lumps had formed on the other breast, she slowly and quietly started putting aside her denial. She began to fortify herself by working out with the weights of acceptance. It was backbreakingly hard work, but it paid off and we were to see (and be amazed at) the refinement dying gave to the quality of her mind and soul.

I came to understand, a long time after my mother's death, that besides being a temporary state of mind, denial also has another disturbing element: You simply don't know you are in denial until you start coming out of it! Hindsight, not foresight, tells you the truth. It's strange but true.

Also, no one person can force another out of denial. Denial has a frustrating way of coming and leaving on its own terms. Always in its own timing—as it did with my mother.

Looking back on my own life, I found that I was in denial about any number of things and was unaware of the blinders denial put over my eyes and soul. When death, losses, or broken relationships became too painful to deal with, and I couldn't cope with issues, I was without hope. It became relatively easy to unknowingly slide into denial. When the reality was too awful or too painful, it was an "easy out" to reach for my "Blue Blanket" to bring the sweet relief of denial.

Then there's the matter of the guilt and fears Christians have over not being absolutely "gloriously victorious" when it comes to death, losses, and suffering. And somewhere along the line we've been led to believe that as Christians, if we are right with the Lord, we will not experience doubts, question God, or have any denial or cover up. But that's not true.

We Christians do not have some kind of supernatural immunity or insurance policy that protects us from feeling the devastating painful blows that come from the tragedies and sufferings of our lives. And it is no sin to slip into denial when the pain is overwhelming.

There is a healthy way of dealing with denial. Step one is to acknowledge the problem. Second, we need to accept the hurts that are encouraging denial as being part of the system here in an imperfect world. Third, we need to put our suffering to work and help others who are broken as we are broken. But as I said, it is not easy to see denial when we are in it.

I remember a fantastic woman of God who talked with me many months after her daughter was killed in an automobile accident. Her daughter, Beck, had driven to work in a neighboring town as usual. At what she thought was a four-way stop, she pulled out in front of a cement truck. The truck hit her car, Beck was thrown out, and the truck crushed her, instantly, into God's presence.

Her mother sat across the table from me after one of my speaking engagements. "What upsets me most," she said, "is that when I was told Beck was dead, I did a horrible thing."

"What horrible thing?" I asked.

"Well, you know. Christians are supposed to be calm and say nice Scripture verses. I didn't. I got hysterical. Why wasn't I able to be like the wife of one of those missionaries who were killed by the Auca Indians of Ecuador? When Betty Saint heard her husband was dead, she quoted Romans 8:28 ["All things work together for good to them that love God, to them who are the called according to his purpose" (KJV)]. She *acted* like a Christian."

I was burning with shame for myself and for any Christian who had ever set up such false standards for Christians. Here was a mother reacting to the sudden death of her daughter in a most normal, human way, yet we church people, the

Christians, had set up phony standards that created her enormous guilt.

"First of all," I began, "let's talk about the missionary's wife. She knew, before her husband and the other four missionaries left on that airplane, that they were about to make contact with men who were part of a well-known headhunter's tribe. The danger was real and the risk enormous. The wives knew what life-defying odds their husbands were facing.

"In your case, though, you had no such risk attached to saying good-bye to Beck that day. There was nothing to indicate it would be anything but an ordinary and rather routine trip to work.

"Secondly, back to the missionaries: The first radio transmission they missed indicated trouble. By the second, and then the third, at half-hour intervals, there was not much doubt that serious trouble had ensued. The wives were, at that point, dealing with their denial, and God was giving them the death knowledge very gradually to help their acceptance. It is not any surprise, knowing the caliber of these dedicated men and women and understanding the dangerous risks involved, that when the dread message finally came, these women had passed on through the early denial stage and had progressed to a God-given acceptance. By then they were able, by God's strength, to quote Romans 8.

"You on the other hand, had no such series of warnings. You were not granted the death knowledge gradually. Your denial took the form of hysterics, and it has nothing to do with whether you were a strong Christian or a weak one."

"Sudden death," as Stephanie, the young widow, told me, "was easy on John but hard on me." We need denial to help us through the most shocking moments of our painful knowledge.

When I was talking with Dr. White about denial, the sudden-death denial problem came up. He told me the story of a young man and his mother. The son had been hit by a car while riding a motorcycle. He was rushed to the hospital where Dr. White happened to be on duty in the emergency room. The young man was dead on arrival.

The mother was contacted where she worked and told that her son had been in an accident. She left work and hurried to the hospital. Even as she entered the emergency entrance, her system was getting ready for any bad news she might hear. The beginning of denial was activated.

Dr. White met her in the hall and helped prepare her by telling her as much as he knew about the accident itself. He did not say her son was dead. He told the mother about the injuries: ". . . broken arm, possible heavy internal bleeding, and head and body cuts." He left her for a few moments in the hall to give her a chance to digest what she had just heard.

It is too much to ask of a human being to be hit with sudden-death news all in one blow. That's why my friend had such hysterics over her daughter Beck's death. By leaving the mother, even briefly, Dr. White was gently letting her assimilate his grievous message.

In a few minutes, he came back and said quietly to the mother, "It is not going well." He explained what they had done medically and what emergency treatments and procedures had been used. (Even if a patient arrives dead, most doctors immediately use all the emergency treatments and drugs available to try to continue life if at all possible. Sometimes the dead-on-arrival verdict is reversed and a life is medically resurrected because of their efforts.)

They had used oxygen and heart massage, so Dr. White told the mother about it in detail, and then he ended with, "Now we have done everything we can possibly do." Once more he left the mother so his words would do their work of preparation.

When he came back, the mother had been joined by the anxious father, and Dr. White led both of them down a corridor and into a small, private examining room. All of this had taken only a few minutes, but it was desperately needed.

Dr. White said to me, "Even as we walked toward the room both the mother and father already sensed their son was dead." When they reached the room, Dr. White said, "We did all we could to save him, but we couldn't. He is gone." He confirmed what they had "known" for the last few minutes, what they'd hoped was not true. The doctor had told no lies, but he had withheld the information just a few minutes to let the mother prepare herself.

The mother's sobbing broke the tension in the room as she buried her face into her husband's shoulder. Even though her voice was muffled, we can hear the agony of her soul as she said, "Oh, no."

This is the exact moment that being a Christian really counts. We are not removed from denial just because we are God's children, but we should know and recognize denial for what it is. We should use it as it is intended, as a buffer zone, and then move into acceptance. We must not live in denial. Anyone who tries to escape the realities of life and death will not be able to handle the ways of death and dying.

It is sad to see someone who has never moved out of denial into acceptance. I knew a father who was very close to his teenaged son. After the son died of leukemia, the father refused to go to football games. He treated that sport as a sacred memory to his son. He allowed no games on TV, nor did he ever talk sports with anyone. By doing so, he kept himself from living life as his son probably would have wanted him to. By doing so, the father kept denial alive.

There was a widow I knew who stayed in deep denial. She refused to touch her dead husband's things. She kept his den door closed and left the room exactly as he had left it. She left his car as he had left it, refusing to take out his paper and trash on the front seat. She was committing a kind of mental suicide by her denial that her husband was gone, though I doubt she knew it.

Both the grieving father and widow I've just described were Christians, yet they let their fears of death and their

fierce desire to deny death rob them of having any real relationships with people who were alive. This type of denial is
very hard on families and friends, frustrating communication
among them. It also means that those living in denial will be
ineffective in living the abundant life God has promised.

It is not easy to move out of denial toward acceptance. It
is not without its cost and complications. In fact, it's a very
old problem.

Jesus tried so hard to help his disciples over the hurdles of
denial. He told them, repeatedly, that he would be betrayed
and crucified, but they covered their hearts and minds with
the robes of denial. Not too long before his death Mary, the
sister of Martha, poured a very expensive perfume over Jesus'
head. The disciples, blinded by their denial, missed the whole
point of her selfless act. They were indignant because, as they
pointed out, the woman had wasted so much money. They
were full of suggestions about how she could have sold the
perfume and spent the money on the poor.

Jesus simply told them they would always have the poor.
He reminded them of his upcoming death and said (again)
that they would not always have him. Then Jesus verbally
painted a beautiful picture of this woman, Mary, who, at great
cost, had passed through denial into acceptance. He said,
"She has done what she could, and has anointed my body
ahead of time for burial" (Mark 14:8).

There is another chilling aspect about denial. A doctor spe-
cializing in childhood leukemia gave the shocking statistics
that 70 percent of the parents obtain a divorce once leukemia
has been diagnosed in their child. He also stated that, if parents and family accepted and recognized the confirmed diagnosis of leukemia in their child, they responded by trying to
prepare themselves for the extreme burdens of caring for their
sick child. They answered their other children's questions
straight on, and they helped the child himself to know that
he was loved and not being dropped or abandoned because
he had this disease. They were with the child when he died.

However, the story was sadly different for parents who denied the diagnosis and the terminal nature of the disease. The stress of this denial usually produced, if not divorce, a separation, and ultimately kept them away from the hospital when death was imminent.

I remember being very shocked and saddened to learn that in a major children's hospital near my home many babies and children died without a doctor, nurse, or either parent present. They died alone because parents and professional people did not want to get emotionally involved with a bound-to-die child. They died alone because adults deny death for fear of the hurt they might experience after the child has died.

Some nurses who work with these children carry out their various duties with callous indifference. They listen as little as possible and touch only when necessary. How sad, but such is the force of denial. It's as if they do indeed hear the mourning song, but they run blindly from the sound, holding their ears and hoping none of the message will get through their carefully structured blockades.

I have seen terminally ill children in several hospitals, and I can fully appreciate how soul-tearing it is to work around them. Still, it is tragic to let denial rob us of feeling, caring, and loving the dying child.

Dr. James Dobson once told me of a mother who was willing to put down her denial, pick up her own acceptance, and beautifully prepare her little son for his death. She came every day to the hospital to visit her little five-year-old son who was dying of lung cancer. All cancers are painful, but lung and bone cancer have a corner on pain and suffering.

One morning before the mother got there, a nurse heard the little boy saying, "I hear the bells! I hear the bells! They're ringing!" Over and over that morning nurses and other staff members heard him.

When the mother arrived, she asked one of the nurses how her son had been that day. The nurse replied, "Oh, he's hallucinating today. It's probably the medication, but he's not making any sense. He keeps on saying he hears bells."

The mother's face came alive with understanding, and she shook her finger at the nurse, saying, "You listen to me. He is *not* hallucinating and he's not out of his head because of any medicine. I told him weeks ago that when the pain in his chest got bad and it was very hard to breathe, it meant he was going to leave us. It meant he was going to heaven. I told him that when the pain got *really* bad he was to look up into the corner of his room towards heaven and listen for the bells of heaven *because they'd be ringing for him!*"

With that, she marched down that hall, swept into her little son's room, swooped him out of his bed, and held him in her arms until the sounds of ringing bells were only quiet echoes. He was gone.

I see her in my mind's eye, a mother who had undoubtedly experienced denial but was not about to wallow in it herself or delude the child with it. She had rocked her son into the arms of God, both of them knowing the peace of acceptance and both of them hearing the mourning song.

We need denial—but we must not linger in it. We must recognize and use it as God's unique tool. Denial is our special oxygen mask to use when the breathtaking news of death has sucked every ounce of air out of us. Denial eases our bursting lungs by giving them their first gulps of sorrow-free air. We breathe in the breath of denial, and it seems to maintain life. We do not need to feel guilty or judge our level of Christianity for clutching the mask to our mouth. After breathing has been restored and the initial danger has passed, however, we need to not be dependent on it any longer.

I think God longs for us to lay down the oxygen mask of denial and with his help begin breathing into our lungs the fresh, free air of acceptance *on our own.*

4

A Time for Anger

There is a right time for everything:
A time to be born,
A time to die; . . .
A time to lose; . . .
A time to speak up; . . .
A time for hating.
Ecclesiastes 3:1–2, 6–8

For some years now I have been writing down, here and there, incidents or feelings of the moment. I also have a considerable bunch of little spiral or not so spiral notebooks full of my prayer lists to God since 1959. I have written these without the thought of publishing. When I wrote, it was merely as a therapeutic exercise, without editing on my part, and as a record to jog my memory lapses from time to time.

More often than once in a while I did not understand my moods or reactions, but I jotted them down anyway just as they hit me. As I reread these notes, I find that some are remarkably cogent, even complete, and others are rather sketchy. Still others have been done in a kind of ridiculous shorthand that makes them largely indecipherable. I suppose

somewhere in the back roads of my mind I envisioned a future
time when I would reexamine the words and come up with
some reasonable explanations.

I did find one set of notes I had written one night after
attending a funeral. Apparently I'd been overwhelmed by
anger. These were my raw thoughts, as I wrote them.

Everything about the mortuary in my town is carefully
geared to comfort the grieving families and friends of the
deceased. Why doesn't it work on me?

The main chapel with its Spanish-Moorish decor has curved,
arched windows and doorways instead of sharp, angular
abutments, and they all blend into a tolerable softness.

The carpeting is a warm sage green and the beige walls
are decorated with elaborately scrolled, wrought-iron
sconces. Their golden bulbs cast a small, warm glow over
the walls and the thick velvet drapes.

The pews are richly carved wood with padded seats, and
they lend a source of solid security to the hall. In fact,
over the whole place is the light fragrance of stability and
security. It's all been planned and designed to bring words
like "peace" and "acceptance" into meaningful focus.

It's all been wasted on me, because not only did I not
have peace or acceptance this morning, I found I had
tensed up at a pretty fast rate of speed.

I was late getting there, so I stood with the overflow
crowd in the vestibule. For a long time I looked through
the windows into the beautifully appointed chapel and down
the aisle at the flag-draped casket of my friend. When I
could bear that scene no longer, I began concentrating on

the beauty of the flowers. Some flowers had been placed in their containers by hands trained in mechanical precision—they looked very dead, plastic, or both. Others were tenderly arranged with sensitive, talented hands and, even from where I stood, the results were breathtaking. They reminded me of life and the land of the living. They seemed to bring my heart a small measure of comfort, but I grew restless again with a growing sense of anxiety. To make time move, I looked up to study the ceiling. Large chandeliers were hung by delicately worked, yet strong, black chains. They were masterpieces of old-world design. Their filigreed iron cylinders framed the amber-colored glass panels and the small light inside glowed with warmth and charm. Still, they did not ease my tension.

Finally, our minister stepped to the small lectern and I gave him my full effort of concentration. His message was not merely appropriate, it was a masterpiece of rhetoric, held together by truth and rightness. At one place he said, "John would not want to come back now, not after seeing what he's now seen—not after hearing what he has now heard and not now, after knowing what he now knows!"

Yet even understanding the truth of his words and believing them with all my heart did not seem to help. Maybe part of my uneasiness is that sometimes there is a quality of dishonest phoniness, hypocrisy, at a funeral. It can get out of hand. Too many nice, rather untrue, things are said about the deceased. Or too many tears shed for someone we hardly spoke to in his life. Too much evading of the truth. Like this morning. The organist was just terrible, but we said,

"Wasn't the music lovely." However, the soloist was good and his song echoed majestically through a screen into the chapel and out to those of us in the lobby, but my heart was still not comforted.

There was, by now, no slight feeling of anxiety, but rather an electric current of frustration jabbing here and there at my soul. I could feel myself getting angry. In fact, by the time I passed by the side door I was stinging with resentments and anger.

Just outside the door two of the morticians recognized me (I've been the guest soloist there for many funerals), smiled, and said hello. I was so bent out of shape over the utterly abhorrent devastation death does to the living, I barely muttered hello as I brushed past them. It's not like me to be so rude.

All day long I've been angry. In John's case, death came and robbed him of his life. Then, as if death is not content with what it did to John, it hovers over John's wife and children with a sinister smile that simply infuriates me!

No beautiful chapel, flowers, sermon, or song seem to appease or comfort me. I'm mad at everybody—from God right on down to the guys who are covering up John's casket right now.

It was much later, after I'd written these observations and thoughts, that I read about anger in Dr. Kübler-Ross's book, and a little bell rang signaling the beginning of some understanding. As surely as denial is our first reaction to death, anger is our second. Denial moves into anger, especially in the terminally ill, because the reality of dying becomes too pronounced and too obvious to deny. Their attitude goes from "Oh, no, not me" to "Oh, yes" and from there to "Why me?" I can see now how perfectly logical it is to warm up the cold atmosphere of death with the heat of anger.

Aside from the sporadic anger I experienced at John's funeral, my first real bout with anger emerged one hour after my infant son David had died. I have written in *His Stubborn Love* of the beautiful moments just after my husband told me David had died. I'd never felt anything like it, for the presence of God sustained me in an incredible way. I did not write of the hours and days that followed David's death, however, because I had been extremely angry, and I felt guilty about that particular emotion rising out of my little spiritual heart. I had no idea that being angry over my loss was normal or that the anger would pass. I could not write of those angry thoughts then because I was sure other Christians didn't have them. Of course I was wrong, but I wasn't to find that out until many years later.

A half hour after David's death, a nurse gave me a shot. It didn't put me out, but it did seem to take the edge off reality and blunt my emotions. When my husband left I began to realize that I'd never see David again on this side of heaven. The enormity of the fact that I hadn't been allowed to take him in my arms hit me full force, and suddenly the tranquil presence of God began to fade like a mist that might not have been there in the first place. I became fearful as I was sure God had left, too. I knew that fear and loneliness had climbed over the rails of my bed, but when I wasn't looking anger had slipped under the covers with them. A few minutes later one of my doctors abruptly banged through my door, shook my bed, and shoved a clipboard in front of my face. I thought he said, "Here, sign this." I was a bit groggy from the tranquilizer by then, and I couldn't hear him too well, so I asked him what he said, and he repeated, "Sign this."

"What is it for?" I asked.

"It's permission to do an autopsy."

With angry, stinging tears pouring down my face, I signed it with the most ridiculous scrawl I'd ever written. He left immediately without a word.

I knew enough about the immense value of autopsies to know that I wanted it done. (David died of internal hemorrhaging due to the Rh-negative blood problem. A couple of years later, medical research would discover answers to the Rh-negative problems, and after that most Rh-babies would not die from those complications. I'm sure that in part, autopsies were responsible for helping doctors find the treatment and cure for this problem.) But they were about to do an autopsy on *my* baby whom I had not even held. And having the autopsy permission papers so crudely and abruptly shoved into my face was devastating. The anger began a slow burning within me.

It was then that the loss of my little son began to be real. It *had* happened. David was not down the hall in the intensive care area for babies; he was gone. The song of mourning rose to a deafening fortissimo in my ears. It was as if the music had been written and orchestrated only for the percussion instruments and everything was pounding, striking, or clanging together. The only lyrics I could come up with were, "Lord, how come you did that?"

Someone somewhere inside me seemed to be beating out a slow, throbbing rhythm on the tympani drums, and the pulsing sounded like the ugly word *dead*. Dead . . . dead . . . dead. . . . I wanted to scream, "Stop this horrid music! Stop it, or I'll burst with the hideous noise of this." I realized then that I'd leave the hospital with an armful of azalea plants and no baby. I couldn't stop the hot tears which seared and stung my eyes.

I was still crying when within minutes of the doctor's visit a nurse from the baby nursery strode into my room. She took one look at me, put her hands on her hips, and in an indignant voice cried, "You're not ready! Why aren't you ready? You know the procedure. Why aren't you washed and ready?"

"Ready for what?" I mumbled. She threw her hands up in an exasperated what-am-I-gonna-do-with-them gesture, looked at her watch, and gave me a run-down on the drill. "It's 4:30 and time for you to nurse your baby. You signed up to nurse. Remember? Now the babies are ready and coming out. You've got your sheet of instructions! Why aren't you ready?"

I looked up at her for a couple of seconds, and as steadily as I could said very slowly, "My baby is dead."

"Oh!" was all she said as she vanished. Somehow that nurse missed another nurse from the nursery. It seemed immediately this second nurse, two babies in her arms, stuck her head in my room and asked, "Mrs. Landorf, are you ready?"

"No, I'm not. My—"

She cut me off with, "Oh, come on. Hurry up."

"My baby is dead." It had hurt to say it the first time with the other nurse, but saying it again was unbelievably painful.

The nurse backed out my door, saying, "My heavens, Mrs. Landorf, they don't tell us anything around here!"

I was angry and frustrated at both nurses and at the whole mess in general. I nodded and tried to smile at her and then looked at the tiny little bundles in her arms. They were beautiful—but they belonged to someone else.

The next nurse who entered my room had another baby on her arm. She passed my bed without a look in my direction and settled my roommate's baby down into her arms for nursing. I'll never forget the sounds of that room as long as I live. The young mother next to me was saying those dear, unintelligible things one coos over her infant as he nurses, and it ravaged my heart. The baby's contented sucking sounds and little moans of joy came across the room as if they were being transmitted by loudspeakers. I felt as if all the life in me was being crushed out.

The beautiful presence of God, so strong, so comforting less than an hour ago, was now totally gone. My husband was gone. The doctors were gone. David was gone, and I kept wondering why God had chosen this very moment to go, too. I felt exactly as if some mysterious plague had wiped out every living being on the face of the earth but me.

Someone at the head desk got very busy all of a sudden, and in a swish of activity my roommate—along with her baby, bed, and personal things—were hurriedly moved out. Then I was really alone.

The door had no more than closed than it opened, and a minister I knew stuck his head in my room and cheerfully called, "Hi, there!" I was pleased to see him, I guess, but I couldn't set my thoughts straight because of the anger eating me. I was rather quiet, for me. The minister didn't seem to notice. He walked over to me, patted my shoulder, and with a confident smile said, "Well now, Joyce, you have this thing under control, don't you? You have no problems with your baby's death, do you?"

He blew my mind right off its hinges. I thought, *No problems! Are you crazy? One hour ago my baby died. Since then I've been to hell and back. I'm just out of C-section surgery, I wish I were dead instead of David, and I'm so mad at God I can hardly see straight! And here you are, smugly confident that I have no problems. How dare you assume such a thing? You honestly think I'm that strong a Christian and have no problems?*

Then the old bugaboo about "What will people think of me?" took effect. I realized that this minister had put me up on some sort of spiritual pedestal. I was not supposed to have any hang-ups, fears, or anger over death because my name was Joyce Landorf. I didn't want to blow my image, so in answer to his questions . . . I lied.

I looked him in the eye and mouthed the stupid untrue words: "Oh, no problems at all. I'm just fine. My baby is with the Lord and everything is all right."

It was the answer he was counting on, so he patted my shoulder again (as if I'd received an A+ on my test) and said, "Good girl." He slipped quietly out of my room, saying something about letting me sleep. I waited for the door to close, then picked up a glass vase, aimed it at the door, thought better of it, and chose not to throw it.

Why did I lie to him? Why didn't I tell him I was angry? Why *didn't* I throw that vase at him? The guilt I felt for just feeling the anger, in the first place, and lying, in the second place, was thumping loudly inside my mind.

A few years later C. S. Lewis, in his book *A Grief Observed*, explained that day of anger for me. He was describing a woman who had lost her child as a woman made in two parts. She had a "God-aimed eternal spirit" side and in another part of her a "motherhood side." He talked of God being a comfort and a hope to her God-aimed spirit side but not to her motherhood side. He said, "The specifically maternal happiness must be written off. Never, in any place or time, will she have her son on her knees, or bathe him, or tell him a story, or plan his future, or see her grandchild." It seemed as if an extraordinary miracle of understanding broke inside of me as I read his healing words.

I am made in two parts. One part of me responds to God, to his touch on my life, and I love him. I can trust him, and I know that no matter how broken and loused up my world may be, he is in control of me and all that transpires around me. My heart can reason: *My baby is not suffering. After all, my baby is with God. My baby is well, warm, and is being rocked to sleep in the arms of God or one of his angels.* With this part of me I can respond to God's restoration of my soul and experience an unexplainable and uncanny peace. I can start to move toward the difficult task of accepting David's death. Spiritually, I am calm and aware that I'm filled to the brim by the mysterious and inexhaustible song of God's comfort.

The other part of me? Ah, now, that's a different story. What of the human side, the earthly, the feet-on-the-ground part of me? That part of motherhood in me? This side is not comforted—not by a long shot. Am I less a Christian? I don't think so. I am just more a mother-human being at this point in my grief. My dreams are broken. My plans, especially the one to be a great mother to this child now that I know what a walk with God is all about, are canceled. I can have no more babies. I have to move, walk, and live in a world where other babies live on. I have to go back home and to church to face my friend Shirley and her baby, her son, the one born at the same time, at the same hospital, only three rooms away; her son who lives. The mother in me is not ready or willing to do this. I am angry and wonder over and over, "Why *my* baby?" I just want *my* baby.

"Oh," you say, "but just think. David is with the Lord!" I *know* that fact, but my mother-self rises up and screams out with inescapable anger, "Well, you tell the Lord to give him back to me. I want him in *my* arms, not God's." The human side of me is experiencing the normal emotion of anger.

One mother, whose son died of bone cancer on his sixteenth birthday, described her bout with anger. She said that early in her son's illness the Lord had plainly told her that her son (named David, too) would not live. She had at that moment begun preparing herself for his death. As the illness drew toward the end, friends came to the hospital to visit the boy. Over and over again they would talk briefly with the boy and then go out into the hall and break down in tears. The boy's mother would put her arms around them and tenderly comfort *them*.

Many times after she'd soothed her friends' heartaches they would ask her how she held up. How could she be so cheerful and helpful? She said her answer was the same: "Of course I don't want David to die. But he *is* going to. I'm smiling and able to understand the finality of his going, but inside I'm yelling, 'Oh God, he's my beautiful son,' and the mother in me wants him to live!"

She confessed to me that while she loved God with all her heart, her inward screaming at God was the only way she could adequately express her rage. She felt a little guilty about this, but the screaming at God was the only way she could vent her anger.

One well-meaning Christian leader, when he heard me say I was angry with God for my son's death, took me aside and tried to set me straight. "Joyce," he cautioned, "I wish instead of saying you were angry at God—couldn't you say you were *frustrated* . . . instead of angry?"

I thought about his suggestion for a long time but concluded no, I wasn't merely frustrated. I was sorely and surely *angry*. No other word came close. I also realized that the man hadn't yet seen death steal away someone who was very close to him, and that perhaps in time he would rethink his own choice of words.

I can well understand human-part anger. After my mother died, one well-meaning Christian lady wrote, "Always remember, your mother went to be with her Lord. She is probably much happier now." In the margin of that note I'd furiously scrawled, *But I'm not!* The daughter-side of me was reacting with considerable anger.

In another letter received at that same time, my friend Bobbie had written, "Just heard of your loss. No matter how you are prepared—losing a mother is never easy!" In the margin of her letter I wrote, *Right!* Bobbie had understood the daughter-side of me very well!

One woman who had just lost her husband told me that several Christians had said in saccharine sweet tones, "Don't worry, God never takes something away without giving you something better." The widow said she wanted to scream, "Are you kidding? My husband was the best! The very best!" She and I were both *angry*, not frustrated, at the thoughtlessness of people, and her human-part recoiled every time she heard this kind of trite comment.

Joe Bayly's human-father-part was *angry*, not frustrated or upset, when he wrote of his eighteen-year-old son's death. I'm grateful for his honesty about his anger. Joe's books and writings have stirred me and many others to action. He has uplifted my spiritual side to God many times, but the day I read his psalm about his son in *Psalms of My Life*, I learned all about Joe Bayly, the father.

A Psalm on the Death of an 18-Year-Old Son

What waste Lord
this ointment precious
here outpoured
is treasure great
beyond my mind to think.
For years
until this midnight
it was safe
contained
awaiting careful use
now broken
wasted
lost.
The world is poor
so poor it needs each drop
of such a store.
This treasure spent
might feed a multitude
for all their days
and then yield more.
This world is poor?
It's poorer now
the treasure's lost.
I breathe its lingering fragrance
soon even that
will cease.
What purpose served?
The act is void of reason
sense
madmen do such deeds
not sane.
The sane man hoards his treasure
spends with care
if good

> to feed the poor
> or else to feed himself.
> Let me alone Lord
> You've taken from me
> what I'd give Your world.
> I cannot see
> such waste
> that You should take
> what poor men need.
> You have a heaven
> full of treasure
> could You not wait
> to exercise Your claim
> on this?
> O spare me Lord forgive
> that I may see
> beyond this world
> beyond myself
> Your sovereign plan
> or seeing not
> may trust You
> Spoiler of my treasure.
> Have mercy Lord
> here is my quitclaim.

Anger about and paralyzing resentment toward death are so annihilating few of us can barely admit them, much less cope with them. If we can somehow admit to our anger, either verbally to a close friend or in writing as Joe Bayly has, there comes a small amount of healing. But most of us think that our anger gives God and Christians a bad name. As I've said before, we are supposed to be "victorious" in all of this, so how can we in good conscience bad-mouth God by giving vent to our angry emotions?

I think the loudest crescendo point of my angry mourning song was reached for the first time in my life the day of my son's funeral. I was still in the hospital recovering from

C-section surgery. On the morning of David's funeral I asked my husband to please call me from the mortuary as soon as the service was over so I could know how it all went. It was to be a private memorial for David. We had invited our parents, the Landorfs and the Millers; dear friends of ours, the Caulkins and the Moores; and of course our children, Laurie and Rick.

I remember lying in my hospital bed, feeling terribly sad and very alone, yet wanting no interruptions during the time of the funeral. I had asked the head nurse to see to it that no one bothered me from 10:00 to 10:30 that morning. In view of the other mishaps over David's death, they were eager to cooperate, and mercifully I was left to tend my wounds.

At about 10:45 my phone rang, and my husband gave me a running account of the service and all that happened. Laurie and Rick had responded well to Dr. Ted Cole's brief message. Laurie had come prepared to cry, with several colors of carefully folded tissues clutched in her little hands. Near the end of Dick's phone conversation he said a little hesitantly, "There is one thing you should know." When I asked what, he said very quietly, "Your parents didn't come."

As soon as I got my breath back and said good-bye to him I dialed my parents' home number. My heart was racing and pounding nearly out of my chest. My dad answered, and when he asked cheerfully, "How are you today?" I was stunned and cried, "Daddy, how come you and Mother weren't at David's funeral? How come you weren't there?" I said it over several times as if to convince myself it was a valid question. Had they really not come?

"Oh," he chuckled a bit, "we didn't think it was so very important. After all, he was just a baby."

"Just a baby?" My mind instantly froze in disbelief. *No, I thought angrily, he wasn't just any baby, he was your grandson!*

By then my mother had picked up the extension and was asking what was wrong. I told her, and quickly she responded

with, "Oh, Joyce-Honey, we are so sorry." My dad added his
words, "Yes, we are sorry, but you didn't need me in a min-
isterial capacity; you had your own pastor, Dr. Ted."

"I *know* I had Dr. Ted," I shouted, "but I needed you!
You are David's grandparents." My mother said something
about my sister having an important dental appointment that
day, but the percussion instruments in my head were clobbering me with their deafening noise, and what was said next
I can't remember because it was drowned out.

In the end I was crying; I think Dad was crying; I know
Mother was crying; and if the operator had been listening
she would have been crying too, as we all kept saying "I'm
so sorry" over and over again.

I will always remember replacing the receiver on the phone.
It had been an incredible experience, and my anger turned
serious and ugly. I went over and over it in my head.

My folks had not bothered to come to their grandson's
funeral. They were sorry and had asked for my forgiveness.
I had said, "Yes, of course I forgive you"; but when the phone
call had ended and I lay back on my pillow I could feel my
anger boiling inside me. I was nowhere near forgiving them!

Thirty minutes later, by the time my husband arrived back
at the hospital from the funeral, I was vomiting. He called
the nurse and she called the doctor. I was given a sedative,
but within three hours a bladder infection erupted, and my
stay in the hospital was increased by five very long and pain-
filled days.

I could not understand anything that was happening: not
David's death, not my parents' attitude. I had said "I forgive you" to my parents, but why hadn't my body or my
emotions accepted it? Everything inside me was glistening
with angry fervor, and try as I might, I could *not* forgive
totally and felt I'd *never* forget. Anger kept rising in and
around me, and I almost drowned in the mental and physical anguish of it. At odd moments I'd tell myself that I was
making too much of the issue, but then I'd review the facts

and counter that it was unbelievable for my parents not to come to their grandson's funeral. The battle raged within me for days, and the stress of it contributed to my being dangerously ill.

When I was finally released, I left the hospital carrying, as I had suspected, an azalea plant instead of a baby and aching with the high fever of anger raging inside of me.

It was some months later that I realized the bitterness I felt toward my parents was totally consuming my mind. It was corroding away my insides, and I felt something had to be done to stop its devastating effects in my life. I reasoned that I needed to be well and whole in all areas, yet every time I saw my parents all I did was silently scream the question, *Why didn't you come?* After their visits I'd be back down in bed for days desperately ill again.

One day I finally leveled with the Lord. I said, "I'm sorry, Lord (whenever we say it like that, chances are we are not *too* terribly sorry!), but there's no way I can forgive my parents. You know I've tried, but I can't explain their absence at the funeral to my in-laws, to our friends, or to our children, much less to myself. I *cannot* forgive Dad and Mother!"

I'll never forget the quiet, still, small voice that spoke in my living room that day. The Lord filled my heart with these thoughts: *I know you can't forgive them. I made you. I know your limitations. I know you are unable to forgive them. But I can. So let me.*

The angry, pounding music stopped for a bit, or maybe it just quieted down, but in place of that strident beat I heard a soft, gentle melody beginning somewhere outside my room. Did I dare hope?

"Lord," I questioned, "how can you forgive so I'll feel a release from this angry bitterness?"

My child, he answered, *let me simply channel my forgiveness through you. Open your heart and mind to me. Do not try to forgive them on your own. I'll do it through you. It will be my work, not yours.*

I'm not sure, even after all these years, how I opened up all the secret cupboards of my heart and mind, but someway, somehow I did. It was my first moment of quiet peace since that disturbing phone call so many months before. A song of freedom started ringing through my heart and mind, and I sat and breathed in its beautiful, healing message.

A few days later, when I saw my parents, I realized I'd been with them two hours and not once thought of the anguishing day of David's funeral. It felt marvelous to stand back, relax, and let God forgive where I couldn't.

A few months after experiencing God's forgiveness of my anger toward my parents and him, and one year to the day after David's funeral, my aunt called to tell me that Grandpa Uzon had died. I left home that morning and drove to Grandma and my aunt's homes to see what I could do for them. I found Grandma in the living room of her little house built behind my aunt's. She was just standing still, shaking her head from side to side in disbelief.

My grandfather, Peter Uzon, had been not only her husband for over fifty years, but her ears as well. Grandpa had come alone to America from Hungary to start his barber shop, and when he'd saved enough money, he had sent for my Grandma. They were both in their late twenties. Grandma came steerage class from Hungary, bringing with her their two children: my mother (Marion) and my uncle Peter. Not long after the Uzons had settled into a newly built house in Cleveland, Ohio, my grandmother had caught cold from the still-damp plastered walls, and the infection which followed had left her completely deaf. Over their years together, Grandpa became her newspaper reader, her chief interpreter, her radio listener, her TV explainer, her Bible reader, and her main hymn singer.

The night before he died, Grandpa read from their big Hungarian Bible, as was their custom. Grandma joyously followed his lips with her eyes. It was the most happy and treasured part of their day. Then he sang the old gospel song,

"My Heavenly Father Watches Over Me." She ran her fingers across the words in the hymnal. It was their special, private time with each other and with God, their loving ritual and spiritual tradition.

When they went to bed that last night Grandpa gave the little night table between their beds two quick shoves, bumping it against Grandma's bed. It was his good-night signal. She leaned up a bit, as she always did, and looked over at him. He did what he had always done and blew two kisses over to her. She caught them with an elaborate gesture and settled down to sleep.

For Grandma to wake early the next morning and wonder why his bed was empty, only to be told he'd gotten up, awakened my aunt in the front house, and died while he waited in their living room for help, left her dazed. It could not be true. She had missed it all. Worst of all, she hadn't said good-bye. A few hours later when I got there, all she kept saying to me in her broken English was, "Papa gone. Papa go."

When I found that one of my uncles was on a flight from the East and would be staying at Grandma's house, I decided to make myself useful by getting the bedroom ready. Grandma quietly followed me. I took the sheets off Grandpa's twin bed first. I wasn't sure where the soiled laundry went, so I looked at Grandma and gestured the question, "Where do these go?" She nodded her head in her direction, so I tossed the sheets to her. The sheets were midair when she realized exactly what she was catching and why. Disbelief settled over her face and quickly resolved into anger, turning her dark eyes even darker.

She caught the sheets and held them very close for a moment. Her eyes snapping, she looked up at the bedroom ceiling, stamped her foot ever so lightly and said, "Oh, Papa, vy you go and not take me? Huh? Vy?"

She was a great deal angrier nine months later at my mother's funeral. In the last days of my mother's illness Grandma had resigned herself to my mother's dying. She had held up quite well until just after the funeral, as the family was saying their final good-byes.

I saw her standing bent over my mother's casket and fairly hissing a verbal stream of Hungarian downward. When she saw me, she stood up and switched to her fractured English. Pointing at my mother, she said, "*She* was not go. I next." She held up one finger to me. "Papa," she said. Then, the second finger, "Me." And with the third finger pointing to my mother's casket, she said, "*Then* Marion." I can still hear how she pronounced *Marion* in Hungarian.

Then she turned from me and looked down at my mother. Apparently she went from anger to acceptance, because she bent over Mother, whispered something in her ear, kissed her cheek, and said, "To Jesus."

I thought she had made her peace with God and that she was over her anger, but as Grandma passed me she muttered under her breath just so I could hear her, "I seventy-nine year. Time me go, not your muma." Knowing she was free to express anger to me and others in the family, including my mother, seemed to bring Grandma her measure of healing. (She stayed just a little mad at God over this turn of events for the next six years, when he finally agreed with her that it was her turn to go.)

At the beginning of this chapter I quoted the Old Testament passage about having a time for everything. When we become involved directly or indirectly with death and dying, there is a time for doubts, frustrations, and yes, even raw anger; but there comes a time for healing, for faith, and for understanding.

We hear that time heals all wounds. But does it? Over the next years after my mother's death I asked myself how I could help others during their time in the intensive-care wards of sorrow. How could I, as a friend, a daughter, a wife, a mother, hurry up the recovery time of a person in the midst of the rage part of their grief?

After Job, in the Old Testament, had lost all his children,

his stock, his land, and everything that was dear to him, he was visited by three friends. Remember them? They were full of advice, so much so that at one point Job pleaded with them and said, "Let me be free to speak out of the bitterness of my soul" (Job 7:11). But one of his friends impatiently snapped back, "How long will you go on like this, Job, blowing words around like wind?" (Job 8:2). Later, completely exasperated with them and probably angry, Job said, "I am weary of living. Let me complain freely. I will speak in my sorrow and bitterness" (Job 10:1).

I didn't want to be a "Job's friend" to anyone experiencing the crises which surround death and losses. I read Dorothy Parker's poem and thought for a long time about just what kind of friend I'd try to be.

The False Friends

They laid their hands upon my head,
They stroked my cheek and brow;
And time could heal a hurt, they said,
And time could dim a vow.
And they were pitiful and mild
Who whispered to me then,
"The heart that breaks in April, child,
Will mend in May again."

Oh, many a mended heart they knew,
So old they were, and wise.
And little did they have to do
To come to me with lies!

Who flings me silly talk of May
Shall meet a bitter soul;
For June was nearly spent away
Before my heart was whole.

I decided that I must treat the broken hearts I find with gentle, loving respect. I must let them "complain freely," as

Job so eloquently asked of his friends. Peter wrote long ago, "And now this word to all of you: You should be like one big happy family, full of sympathy toward each other, loving one another with tender hearts and humble minds" (1 Peter 3:8).

Today I reread and examined a man in the New Testament named Thomas. But I looked even closer at his friends, Jesus' disciples. I found they were "full of sympathy" toward Thomas and, the Scripture tells us, they loved him with "tender hearts and humble minds." Do you remember this disciple of Jesus who has been referred to, over the years, as "Doubting Thomas"?

In my mind's eye I see him walking along a dirt road to the house where his associates are gathered. Defiantly, with an angry fire burning inside him, he kicks a stone out of his way and watches it as it ricochets off a wall and crushes a small wild flower. He trusted someone and was let down. Now he feels deceived, betrayed, and, if you please, robbed. Just as he believed he had found a bona fide person, this man Jesus— who seemed to have authority, power, and the answer to every one of life's problems—ends up dead. The man who many believed was the long-awaited Messiah was now executed and left nailed on a cross like any common criminal. Thomas concludes that Jesus was a fraud because now the whole world has seen him die. Thomas arrives at the house at the same time he comes to the summation of his problem and thinks, "I've been had." It sends his inner fires of anger out of control. He enters the house and irately lays out his bitterness and wrath in front of his friends and fellow workers.

What comes out of that meeting is, in the end, perfectly beautiful to me:

Thomas's friends do not wash their hands of him because disciples are not supposed to be doubtful or angry.
They do not hush him up and hustle him out a side door.
They do not give him a lecture on the poor quality of spiritual faith he seems to be showing.

They do not give him a pat on the back and tell him he'll
get over this and that time heals all wounds.
They simply say, in great, loving sympathy, "Oh, Thomas,
wait until you see him!"

How dearly we need to have at least one other person be
patient with our doubts!—one other human being who lets
us vent our anger, who tries to understand our point of
view. We don't need anyone to condemn, challenge, or lecture us at this moment. We need a friend who will lovingly
sit with us and help us wait it out—someone to say, "Oh
dear one, wait till you see the Lord!" We need a friend who'll
stay with us.

Many months before her death, my mother slipped out of
denial into anger. Her angry outburst to me over Dale's letter and my Christmas card was the beginning. I knew she was
moving from, "Oh, no, not me . . . I don't have cancer" to
"Oh, dear, *it is me.*" Since God had been a part of her lifestyle
for so long, I wondered if her anger would be directed toward
him. I didn't have long to wait to see it in action.

I was at home one day when I felt strongly that I should
leave everything and go across Los Angeles to Reseda to visit
her. So I switched some things around on my calendar, got
dinner arranged, and drove the hour or so to my parents'
house. When I got there I went down the hall, found her,
and stuck my head into the den.

Mother was in bed, leaning back on the pillows. She had
her eyes closed, and I thought she was asleep until I saw the
smile on her face. I noticed that her hands were folded on
top of an overturned book. I remember I didn't even say
hello, I just softly asked her what had happened. Mother
didn't change her position; she just opened her eyes, looked
at me, and smiling broadly now said, "Oh Joyce-Honey, I've
had the most wonderful experience."

She had been reading a book about Dr. Paul Carlson, a
medical missionary to the Republic of Congo (now Zaire).

She told me she had just been reading that Dr. Carlson was running toward the safety of a stone wall by the mission compound when Congolese rebels shot him to death. The area was liberated fifteen minutes later, but for him it was just fifteen minutes too late. Mother sat straight up in bed in order to tell it better. She said that when she'd come to this part of Dr. Carlson's story, she had put the book down and felt absolutely furious at God for allowing this dedicated doctor to die.

After all, she had mentally shouted at God, *he was only in his thirties. He was a doctor, hard at work for your cause and for healing. Why did you do that to him? Why did you cut him down in the prime of his life and ministry? What mean joke were you playing on him? You let him go to Africa, be useful; and then you have him get shot just as he was about to reach the safety of the stone wall?*

As I looked at her she lay back down against the pillows. I thought I heard a trace of sweet sorrow touching her voice when she said, "Of course, Joyce-Honey, what I was really downright mad about was the question of why had God allowed me to have such a ministry, one that was so blessed by his touch, and then why was he taking me? Why now?" It was the first time that I had heard her, in her very own words, admit that she knew she was terminally ill. The moment tore me apart.

"Don't cry, honey," she said. "Do you know what the Lord answered me about my questions on Dr. Carlson?" (I should have known he'd answer her!)

"No, what?" I asked.

"Well, the Lord seemed to be saying, *Marion, you think Dr. Carlson was busy and effective for me and my work there in the Congo? Oh, Marion, you should see him now!* My mother's eyes were glistening with tears, and she continued, "Then Joyce-Honey, the Lord said, *Marion, my dear child, you think you're busy there in Reseda, California? Just wait till you get here!*"

It was Victor Hugo who said:

> My life has not ended,
> I shall begin work again in the morning.

When I read that I recalled that beautiful scene in the den with my mother that day and wondered about all the "work" she has done since September 1966.

She had expressed her outcry of anger at the Lord. She had recognized it and dealt with it head-on. Though it had taken time, the wounds of anger were clean cuts. The cuts were well on their way to healing because they were not infected with the pus of bitterness or self-pity.

God had not been shocked at her outburst, nor did he punish her or send down a bolt of lightning at her for her resentment. He used her anger as an opportunity to give her a hope-filled message. He used the emotions she was feeling to tell her clearly that her past work was not finished, as she thought, but just about to begin in earnest. She could lose her anger within the confines of God's loving message. She spent her anger that day and I was never to see, hear, or feel anger in her again.

I am so glad our Lord understands our anger at death and dying, and I suspect when he was hanging on the cross it was the emotion of anger that fired off the words, "My God, why hast thou forsaken me?" Anyone who has experienced the agony of a loved one's dying or stood by the dying relates well to the anger in Jesus' voice when he said those words. Jesus' one word *why* is the angriest word in that sentence. Again, we can identify because at one time or another we have pondered and struggled with the whys of things, even to the point of being angered by those fearful whys.

This morning a letter came from a terribly distraught pastor's wife. One line says, "Oh, Joyce, if only God would tell me the whys of this situation, I'd be able to understand it better." But I wonder: would she? Would you? Would I?

I certainly wish I had some brilliant answers to the whys of life and death, but I don't. There is a comfort in the fact that neither does anybody else. There are a great deal of things in life that are complex, contradictory, and go way beyond our ability to ever understand them, yet we must go on living.

I do not understand how electricity works, and I'm not too sure Edison did, either. Yet electricity sustains and maintains life for me and my family. It is also the same force that electrocuted the life *out* of a telephone lineman yesterday. I hate the conflict here, and I do not pretend to understand it, yet I have to live with it and move on. I must use the electric current in spite of its dangers.

In the same way, I do not know the whys of life and of a loved one's death, but I must carry on with the living. I don't enjoy anger as part of life's current, nor am I proud of this emotion, but I must understand that it's a natural response to the bad things that happen. When we don't understand life's circumstances is when trusting God becomes paramount, for that trust enables us to endure with faith.

God can, and often does, give us just enough hope or intervention to whet our appetite for life. He can feed our inner hungers and heal our emotions without specific, authoritative answers.

Sometimes our faith is stronger than our endurance, and in these times God's presence shines like a twenty-five-foot Christmas tree trimmed with one light for every tiny branch. I am dazzled by the sight whenever I see it glowing out of one who is grieving. Other times, the lights of our faith burn low, flicker, and almost go out. Then we have to hang on to the handle of our endurance. If we let go, we will surely fall, so we must *hang on*.

Christ was definitely hanging on to life while he was dying. Yet he gave his own death tremendous dignity. What was, even by its name *crucifixion*, ugly, gross, violent, and horror-filled, he turned into awesome grandeur. With his bones out of joint, all muscles tearing and burning, and probably with an infectious fever raging out of control, he looked, saw his mother, and delegated John to see to her needs. Our Lord was angry; he expressed it; but he did not stay in anger. He moved on to lovingly take care of others in those moments. Such love, such remarkable love, offset one of the world's violent moments in history.

We may never know the answers to all the whys or the hows of death, and certainly we may not be able to completely cope with our anger when it surges and rages, but God is in command. Someday there will be no anger and no dying, for God will put an end to death forever. So until then, *there is a time for anger.* We must deal with it, recognizing it and getting help from God and others so that we can move on, move through it, and move out of its crippling atmosphere.

As Christians we can choose to move out of anger without guilty regrets, even when our anger has been directed at God. He is not surprised or shocked by our anger; after all, he put that emotion inside us just as he did joy and hope. As believers we know that we serve a God who understands us. We can move, breathe, and even sing again because of our faith, our God-given endurance, and our heaven-sent hope of everlasting life.

5

Striking the Biggest Bargain of All

Spare me, Lord! Let me recover and be filled
with happiness again before my death.

Psalm 39:13

On Christmas Day in 1965, my mother was so ill from the
cobalt (radiation) treatments she had undergone that she
hardly moved off the couch except briefly to sit at the dinner table and pick at her food. Yet somewhere between Christmas Day and the second week of January she experienced
what she felt was a miraculous encounter with God.

Mother phoned me one rainy day in January, and immediately I was fascinated by the exuberant tone of her voice. I
could hardly believe the change. She sounded like her old
joyous, radiant self, and her words rushed out, tumbling
enthusiastically over one another.

"Oh, Joyce-Honey," she explained, "I asked God to heal
me and to give me fifteen more years to live. I know deep
down in my heart that God wants me to be healthy and so,
well, I trusted him for a complete healing." She paused. "*He*

89

did it! You know how sick I was at Christmas? Well, now I feel absolutely marvelous!" She finished her report with a glorious ring of authority in her voice.

My heart took a couple of giant flip-flops, and I couldn't find my voice, so I didn't respond. I was stunned. The incredible had happened! She had actually bargained with God for a fifteen-year miracle, and by the sound of her voice, I was sure she'd gotten it! God had heard her, and she'd won the prize!

The doctors at UCLA Medical Center had started Mother on the chemotherapy 5-FU (fluorouracil) treatment only a few days before, so it was hard to believe the treatment had worked so well and so quickly. Yet here she was talking to me with no traces of fatigue or pain coming through. She sounded very healthy, like her old self; and the familiar lilt, almost like singing, rang through her voice.

Dr. Elisabeth Kübler-Ross listed three ingredients her research had indicated were present when anyone bargains for more time:

1. The bargain includes a prize offered "for good behavior."
2. It sets a self-imposed deadline.
3. It includes an implicit promise that the patient will not ask for more if this one postponement is granted.

A strong Christian, my mother had definitely bargained with the Lord in prayer using those three rules. First, she had reminded God that she'd served him her whole life, and she promised now that if he healed her she would vigorously resume teaching her Bible classes and tell her story as a testimony of God's faithfulness to us. She would also give him all the credit and glory.

Second, since she was about to turn fifty-seven, she asked for just fifteen more years. "After all," she said to me, "hasn't God promised us seventy years?"

Third, she promised the Lord that she would die willingly in fifteen years and not ask for a moment more. She was sure she would not ask for more time because, as she explained to me, "By then your sister and brother will be married."

Mother had with great faith marched lovingly into God's presence and struck her bargain for fifteen more years. We phoned each other all during the month of January, and she sounded stronger with every call.

The first week of February drizzled and rained itself into California that year, and with it came my mother's birthday and mine. But nothing could dampen her belief that God had heard her bargaining pleas and granted her request. Her birthday card to me had her special handwritten message.

My dearest,

My every prayer and wish in a daughter has been met— in you. I ask for nothing more but that you continue in life with spiritual success, health, joy, and peace.

What a joy to belong to Him and each other. I'm so thankful for the blessed fellowship we have with one another.

And just think—praise be to our Loving Savior—we are both well and enjoying our birthdays!

Love,
Mother

Toward the end of that week I was driven to Ruth Harms Caulkin's home in Pomona and surprised by a gathering of women. As it turned out, it was a birthday luncheon in my honor. As I came in the door of Ruth's home, I glanced around and saw not only several close friends, but their mothers as well. Out of the corner of my eye and to the right of me, I thought I saw my mother. I turned to get a direct view into the living room and did indeed see my mother! She was standing there in a navy-blue knit suit trimmed in red and white, looking for all the world like a radiant, beautiful picture of health. I just stared at her for a few moments, because the last time I'd seen her was on Christmas Day when she had been very weak, obviously dying, with her skin cancer-colored gray.

Yet there Mother stood, arms outstretched, waiting to welcome me. She had never looked more beautiful to me. It is a picture I've held onto all these years. It's what I feel she looks like today in heaven. Her hair had just been done, and her eyes were sparkling; her skin was lineless, and it had returned to her creamy, healthy beige color. She was so beautiful. I stumbled over to her, cried, hugged and kissed her, and could not believe my eyes. It was unreal.

"No," she claimed, "it's a miracle."

The day after the birthday party, she wrote me a note. It said:

> My dear Ones,
>   Praise God for the beautiful day that met my eyes when I awakened at 9:00 a.m. today.
>   I enjoyed yesterday so very much. I love my gifts—I'm going to wear and enjoy each one.

Her letter went on as she told me of some family pictures she was sending and that my sister, Marilyn, was listening to *The Sound of Music* album. Then she closed the letter by saying:

> I must close and get the roast in the oven. Next Monday I go to UCLA Medical Center again—quite a routine! But thank God, I'm feeling so very good. On Wednesday I'm going to prayer meeting and giving my testimony of healing and I'll praise God for all of it.

Did you know—Christ in you—that means "life"?—and
I have Him and by His life—I have life!

Lovingly,
Mother

I saw her a day later and again was stunned by her healing. I thought, *She's actually struck that bargain with God!* It
looked for all the world as if cancer had been completely
defeated.

After our visit I received this note:

My dearest Joy,

How was your day on Sunday? I pray it has been a success and a blessing.

I was at UCLA today. Things are still the same. Praise
God! I'm feeling great. I'm even anxious to get out and
go shopping a little. [Shopping was her favorite indoor sport.]

A famous doctor is lecturing at UCLA Medical Center
to several doctors. I was asked if I'd be willing to let
them see and examine me. They said my case is remarkable
and of course I think so too. Oh, I'm so grateful and thankful to my loving Savior.

It's 11:00 p.m. and my bedtime. I'll say goodnite. Kisses
to my children and Rickie and Laurie.

Love always,
Mother

Later that week, when I visited her at her home, she was
still bubbling enthusiastically. Her vivacious spirit was alive
and well. She had just returned from UCLA and had been
questioned and on display for some world-famous cancer spe-

cialists. Mother's main doctor had discussed at great length her remarkable improvement. Much of the talk was too medically scientific for her to understand, but at the end of the session they showed her the medical charts they kept on her. At the bottom of the last page were written the words, "Dramatic recovery."

We talked for a long time that day about what had happened in the past weeks. Again she told me about Christmas, when she was so ill, and how she had begged God to heal her. About that time, many Christian friends had been seeing her or phoning and telling her that God wanted her to be well, and only Satan wanted her to be sick. She *should be well*. Over and over in those weeks she heard:

"God can heal cancer."
"You should go to a healing service and ask So-and-So to
    pray for you."
"You should stop eating meat and go on a grapefruit diet."
"You should go to Mexico and get the famous laetrile
    cancer-curing treatment."

One woman pressured Mother by saying, "Mayo Clinic has a secret cure for breast cancer," and that she would pay my mother's way there. (Hearing that one I phoned Dr. Ralph Bryon, the chief surgeon at City of Hope Hospital in Duarte, California, and asked if that were true. He answered, "If it *was* true it would be no secret. Mayo Clinic, Hope, UCLA, and every other clinic and hospital in the world would have it available to their patients.")

Many well-meaning Christians, in great love, unknowingly rocked my mother's world severely between Christmas and Valentine's Day that year. It was almost as if she had to have a miraculous healing to prove there was a God. She also was expected to be healed to prove that her love, faith, and trust in God were alive and well, and that his forgiveness of her was up to date. She especially had to prove it to the lady in their church who insisted Mother must be sinning. "No one gets cancer, my dear Marion," she snidely mentioned to Mother, "unless there is sin in their life!"

I wish I'd known at that moment that Mathew Henry had written of dreadful diseases as "spiritual promotions." He said:

> Extraordinary afflictions are not always the punishment of extraordinary sins, but sometimes the trial of extra-ordinary graces. Sanctified afflictions are spiritual pro-motions.

As I've already said, not even medical science knows what makes a latent cancer cell suddenly erupt in a violent storm of activity. Also, theologically we have been taught that death and dying come because we all have been exposed to the germ of sin spawned way back in the Garden of Eden. We all have sinned, the Scriptures say, and ever since that fateful day in the lives of Adam and Eve we have been experiencing the diseases of life, and steadily we have been dying from them.

I also now know my mother wasn't the first or the last who was pressured by questions such as, "Which sin have you committed?" or "Where is your faith?" For many decades people in physical, emotional, or spiritual pain have been degraded and deeply hurt in this manner. It is with deep sorrow I have to report to my brothers and sisters in Christ that people without God rarely ask these questions. Usually it's believers who ask them of other believers.

The young mother who shared her experience with me about her fifteen-year-old son's death from cancer had had her experiences with well-meaning Christians, too. She related to me that very early in her son's treatment she had prayed for her son's healing. She pleaded and bargained with God to heal him of cancer. The mother did not recall the exact words of the Lord, but when God did speak to her, the words had boiled down to a quiet *no*. The mother's prayer time ended peacefully, but she knew that the answer from God had been definitely, *No. Your son will not get better. He will die.*

From that moment on, in what I consider remarkable maturity, this mother began to change the agenda of her praying. Now she prayed (1) for her son to have more pain-free moments; (2) for her son's good relationship with Christ to get even better; and (3) for her son's witness at the hospital with doctors, nurses, and staff, and at home with his brothers and sisters.

Interestingly enough, when this woman stopped trying to bargain with God, began to deal with the facts, and changed her prayers, she felt that God immediately began to answer these prayers with large *yes*es. She said her own peace of mind was incredible. What's even more important, the woman felt that she had achieved the hard-earned goal of accepting her son's death without a trace of morbidity or bitterness. The woman and her husband and family did just fine. Just fine, that is, until the word got around in their church that they were not praying for their son's complete healing of cancer.

Slowly at first and then faster came the criticism from other church members. She was accused of not trusting God, of doubting that God could heal, and worst of all, of displaying a shocking lack of faith in God.

Mentally and spiritually she was bewildered by their cold, ostracizing reactions. To her, it seemed as if God were doing incredibly beautiful things *through* her son's cancer, not his healing. This mother felt that God had plainly told her that her son would not live but was approaching death. Yet to most of her friends at church, accepting his dying as God's answer to her prayers somehow made her a traitor, guilty of spiritual treason.

She described the ongoing nightmare and related that the whole thing came to a dreadful boiling point when several pastors and some deacons from her church came unannounced to her home and insisted that they'd come to pray for her son's complete healing. Tearfully, she tried to explain to them that the doctors' medical opinions and her own prayerful conclusions were that in her son's case the cancer was terminal. She felt heaven would bring the ultimate healing for her son. She asked them not to pray that he be well, but to pray for what would probably be the last months of his life. She reminded them that her son was a dedicated, even radiant, Christian teenager. Also, she told them, he had already accepted with great dignity and joy his serious disease and had anticipated dying and being with Jesus.

This mother then related some of the miracles God had done in the lives of the hospital staff and those who stood at her son's bedside. Seeing no acceptance on the faces of the men gathered in her living room, she desperately begged them to pray in these directions.

I am still saddened and even feel angry every time I think about the response of those sincere men of God. They were disgusted with her for what they saw as her lack of faith, and they told her they were ashamed of her for not believing that God could heal cancer. They abruptly left her home. What really dug itself into the innermost part of my soul was her next sentence. She said, "You know, Joyce, for the many months of my son's illness and until the time of his death, not one of those ministers ever came to my house or visited my son at the hospital again."

We Christians can be so sure about the puzzle pieces of God's plans, so sure about the direction of God's ways, and so sure about the way God's mind is working that it is possible for us to completely miss his bona fide miracles cracking and popping like bright bolts of lightning all around us.

When Jesus walked this earth he healed many, many people. He even healed Lazarus from death. But what of the thousands he did *not* heal? Was it because of their sins that he didn't heal them, to punish them? I don't think so. I know from my own sojourn that God allows suffering, and yes, death. But I cannot believe that my heavenly father sits on his high throne, holds us like little voodoo dolls in his hand, and pokes pins and needles into us just to punish us for our sins.

When will we understand that sometimes, more often than not, God's healing is not meant for here on this earth, but for heaven? Oh, I'm not saying he doesn't heal here. I know this fact personally for he has on many occasions healed me, sometimes even miraculously. But we must be cautious about making blanket statements about his healing.

When the pastors told the mother to pray for her son's healing and she refused, these Christian brothers tried, convicted, and sentenced her for not praying *their* way and for her "lack of faith" in accepting God's healing.

Joe Bayly wrote in *The View From a Hearse*, "Death for the Christian should be a shout of triumph, through sorrow and tears, bringing glory to God, not a confused misunderstanding of the will of God to heal."

Not long ago a woman twice widowed shared with me her experience when she bargained with God about healing her husband so he would not die of cancer. She had lost her first husband after thirty years of marriage. Two years later she had married again. They had seven wonderful years together. Then he got cancer.

She told me of their happiness and that she had felt seven years was too short a time together. So she had pleaded and bargained with God to completely heal her husband. The woman related that when he was very close to dying, she knelt by his bed and begged the Lord for his healing. She said the Lord's voice spoke so clearly to her that she was quite startled by it. She heard him say very distinctly in her heart and mind, *My child, your husband has prepared himself to accept death and to die right now. Tell me, do you want him to prepare himself again, later on?*

She said that at this point she opened her eyes and took a good look at her beloved husband. He was at peace. He had reached an obvious acceptance of death. She said, "Oh, Joyce, I knew right then I'd have to let him go. It wouldn't be fair or human of me to make him go through that again later on, so I released him. In that instant, a great peace settled over me. He quietly died a few hours later, and *both* of us were at peace."

Think about this: If she had clung to her bargaining mode and begged God to let her husband live, she would have missed what God wanted to do in their lives. Instead, she released her husband into the arms of God and began being the woman God wanted her to be. She told me how grateful she was for those marvelous seven years, how sad she was that he was gone, and how she missed him—but how alive and excited she was about living today and for whatever time she would have here.

She was a very different woman from the one I read about in Charles L. Allen's book *When You Lose a Loved One*. He told of a woman whose husband was dying. In fact, the doctor had said he was gone. The children became hysterical and begged their mother to pray. So she knelt down, prayed, and asked God to bring her husband back to life. The man opened his eyes, recovered, and lived nine more years. Mr. Allen wrote, "But those nine years were for him so painful and unhappy that no less than a thousand times did she regret that God answered her prayer."

We love to talk about Jesus raising Lazarus from the dead. But we rarely consider the fact that at a later date Lazarus *died*. He did not live forever. We don't know how many years his miraculous stay of death lasted, but we can know for certain he did at some time die. I wonder how his health was during those years, but I particularly wonder what Martha's and Mary's thoughts were when he died a *second time*. If I ever write a sequel to *I Came to Love You Late*, my novel about Mary, Martha, and Lazarus, it will be of the years after his rescue from death.

I have always believed, with all my heart, in divine healing. God can heal, if he chooses, any illness. A God who made us in the first place can most certainly heal all our diseases.

During my mother's illness, though, I fell into the trap of restricting God to only one kind of healing. Over the years, I have learned that God heals in many ways and is not narrowly limited to only one method. Listed here are only four of his ways.

1. Spontaneously

During my mother's illness in the '60s, I thought God's healing was *only* done spontaneously. I have personally experienced physical healing. On at least three occasions in my childhood my parents prayed over me during a desperate illness. Instantly and spontaneously I was well. Many other times when the illness was not too serious, they would pray only for my fever to drop, and by the next day I would be completely recovered. Other people I have known have gone to healing services in a church or to a gathering of praying people, and God has instantly healed them.

So I've been acquainted with God's instant healing for a long time, but when I talked with my healthy-looking mother in January about her miraculous healing, something about it disturbed me. I grew uneasy when she kept repeating, "God has completely *cured* me." For some reason the last three words of that statement, particularly *cured*, were difficult to swallow; they stuck in my throat like small, irritating fish bones. I felt guilty immediately about this because it seemed to indicate a lack of faith on my part. Why couldn't I accept the word *cured*? Why wasn't I simply ecstatic with joy and thanksgiving? What was the matter with me? Didn't I believe God could heal? Of course I did. So what was my problem?

After visiting Mother one day in February of that year, I drove home in the slow lane of the freeway. It took almost an extra hour to get to my home, but I deliberately drove slowly, as it gave me the necessary time to sort out what I'd seen and heard. My thoughts and emotions heaved and rumbled within me.

Obviously, I reasoned, she looks, acts, and feels cured. No way could I argue with that kind of visual and emotional success. I knew God had healed her spontaneously, but—and for the first time a new thought about healing rose up in my mind—what if she had not been cured, but only been given a remission—a reprieve or a stay of execution? I wondered if that was healing of a different sort. If that were true, I quickly figured, at best her improvement would be temporary. These thoughts ate like acid through my heart. I headed my car into the fastest lane in the center of the freeway and shoved the accelerator down hard for the last few miles before my turnoff.

The California February rained itself into March that year, but my mother walked in nothing but blue skies and pure sunshine. Her health was never better.

April found us happily shopping occasionally, as we loved to do. My mother resumed teaching her Bible classes, and they were filled with overflowing crowds of women eager to learn. Many women, some long estranged from God, found their way into her classes, and with my mother's sensitive and warm introduction that was only hers, they met her friend, the Lord and Savior Jesus.

The twelfth of May brought Mother's Day around, and she sent a card to me. It was signed (rarely just "Mother"), "From a loving mother who is proud and grateful for such a precious daughter." I flipped the card over and read on the back page:

My dearest Joyce,

I didn't think at one time back a few months ago that, I would live to enjoy Mother's Day with my loved ones.

But here I am—better and stronger—and in no pain whatever! Praise God!

I shall never cease to praise Him for His touch on my body and the marvelous miracle of healing performed. My prayer is that I may be worthy of His love and serve Him with joy with my new health and strength. And I thank Him for my dear, dear children. May He bless and keep you all.

Always with love,
Mother

I thought, *Well, that's that. I can't argue with that kind of evidence. Mother was right. She is cured. It was wrong of me to have doubts. She has experienced spontaneous healing.* I felt she had bargained with God and received her extended fifteen years.

In those ecstatic days Psalm 116 became my mother's source of proof. I'm not sure, but I suspect she memorized it. Obviously, David had experienced the bargaining stage because he described it very aptly.

Death stared me in the face—I was frightened and sad. Then I cried, "Lord, save me! How kind he is! How good he is! So merciful, this God of ours!" The Lord protects the simple and the childlike; I was facing death and then he saved me. Now I can relax. For the Lord has done this wonderful miracle for me. He has saved me from death, my eyes from tears, my feet from stumbling. I shall live! Yes, in his presence—here on earth! In my discouragement I thought, "They are lying when they say I will recover." But now what can I offer Jehovah for all he has done for me? I will bring him an offering of wine and praise his name for saving me. I will publicly bring him the sacrifice I vowed I would. His loved ones are very precious to him and he does not lightly let them die.

Psalm 116:3–15

My mother was also very familiar with a man named Hezekiah in the Book of Isaiah. Since she taught Old Testament and knew it like the back of her hand, she had used this passage in her bargaining with God. She knew that Hezekiah was told by the Lord, "Set your affairs in order, for you are going to die; you will not recover from this illness" (Isa. 38:1). She knew that when he got this news bulletin he turned his face to the wall and bargained like mad with God. He reminded God of how he'd served and obeyed him, and then he just "broke down with great sobs" (Isa. 38:3).

Mother also knew Hezekiah had been heard by God and was given years more to live. Right! It was fifteen years, to be exact. She rationalized her breast surgery and illness exactly as Hezekiah had when he wrote a poem about his illness. Among other things, he said:

> Yes, now I see it all—it was good for me to undergo this bitterness, for you have lovingly delivered me from death; you have forgiven all my sins. For dead men cannot praise you. They cannot be filled with hope and joy. The living, only the living, can praise you as I do today. . . . Think of it! The Lord healed me!
>
> Isaiah 38:17–20

My mother recounted Hezekiah's experience to anyone and everyone who would listen and rejoiced that it was her experience, too. She *knew* she had fifteen more years.

But my doubts wouldn't lie down and be quiet. There was never a more confusing time in my life than those months with my mother while I tried to sort out my feelings and emotions regarding healing. Actually, my passing thought that God might have other ways of healing was the key, but not until long after her death did I fully realize that. It was as if the Lord sorted it out for me then.

2. Gradually

Eventually I was to understand that God heals not only spontaneously, but also gradually.

I recalled a time that I had surgery. I'd had the finest doctors; even several specialists had been consulted. I received top-notch nursing care, concentrated intensive care; everything had been geared to get me through the surgery and meet my recovery needs.

Looking back on it, I find it apparent that after the doctors had done their best work, after the surgery tools were sterilized and put away, everyone, including me, had to wait. Nothing more could be done. We all had to enter God's waiting room and sit for the time it would take for gradual healing to happen.

I talked to Dr. Jim White about this gradual type of healing God performs. He told me of praying before each surgery and that his prayer was for the Lord to give him all the skills and wisdom his training had given him to be put into use.

"However," he said, "I learned early in my practice that as a surgeon I could relieve and heal *pain* in my patients, but only God could heal *suffering*. After I've done my best work, I always have to stand back, wait, and watch. Only God can heal the body and the mind and make recovery possible."

I asked him if he had ever heard a patient bargaining for more time. He smiled and said, "No, not directly, but I remember one patient I *definitely* bargained over with God." In this particular case he had prayed as usual before surgery. He had operated and felt all was progressing routinely well. Three days after the operation, the patient's progress reversed itself, and the man's condition started to deteriorate. Neither Dr. White nor his staff could find any rhyme or reason for the situation. The man's condition continued downward, and finally, thirty days after what had been a routine surgery, the patient was comatose and obviously in the throes of dying.

Dr. White said, "That day I went before the Lord and bargained with God to give this man's life back to him. I told the Lord I would level with the family and give God all the honor if he would only spare this man's life." Amazingly the man began the gradual recovery process. Dr. White went to the family and said, "As a doctor I had done everything I could possibly do, and yet he was dying in spite of all our work. I want you to know I asked God to raise him up and God answered my prayer. I'm telling you this because I promised God I'd give him the honor. It was his doing, God's miracle, not mine." Dr. White's story is an example of how God granted a gradual healing.

3. Circumstantially

God also heals circumstantially. That's exactly the type of healing that had taken place in the lives of the mother and her dying teenaged son. God did not heal her son or take away the bone cancer, but he healed people and a great many circumstances all around the boy. God healed the mother's and father's anxious, troubled hearts. He healed the grieving hearts of the brothers and sisters by giving them a genuine peace. And during her son's hospital stay, God healed some doctors, nurses, technicians, and many other staff people.

My millionaire friend Mary Korstjens, the beautiful lady I wrote about in *The Richest Lady in Town*, is the recipient of circumstantial healing. God has not healed her of polio or taken away her from-the-neck-down paralysis. But he has brought circumstantial healing to Mary; her husband, Keith; her family; and scores of people around her. Every once in a while a group of Christians will with great faith and sincerity pray for Mary's healing from paralysis. What they miss is the important fact that she has already experienced healing in ways that are not physical.

Von Letherer, my friend who represented me for speaking engagements and to whom this book is dedicated, was returned to the hospital for treatments at the time of this book's first writing. A day or so after his return I talked with his wife, Joanne, who said, "Of course we have always wanted God to completely heal Von of his disease. But I wonder, if God had healed Von years ago and made him well, wouldn't we have missed all the amazing miracles God wanted to share *through* Von's being a hemophiliac? I think so. And I also think Von is the special man of God he is because he has allowed God to lead him throughout his whole life for all these years, in spite of his pain and sickness." Von and Joanne are still living their lives within the framework of circumstantial healing.

4. Temporarily

There is a fourth way God heals. This is the type of healing medical science calls a remission. Some remissions are incredible. In leukemia, as in other cancerous diseases, patients experiencing a remission can live with practically no symptoms of the disease. They can lead fairly normal lives for weeks, months, or even years. The disease appears to have stopped all its activity or growth, and the patient resumes a life clinically free of the disease.

I was familiar with the word *remission* during my mother's illness, but I did not consciously think of it as being a viable healing from God. In my subconscious, though, my mother's wellness was beginning to take the shape of remission. I felt a little guilty for not trusting God for a cure.

I was starting to think, just barely, about the possibilities of her remission when one day I asked Mother if she thought God had cured her, or was she in—I tried to phrase it delicately—a medical remission? She went completely out of character and instantly grew cold and distant. Distinctly, she stated, "No remission. God's *cured* me," adding, "you'll see."

I felt some small cactus needles pricking the back of my mind. I felt them again when my dad handed Mother a gift he had bought her. It was a beautiful, leather, lady's attaché case. She held it up and happily said, "Oh, look at this! It's for my notebooks to take to my Bible study classes. I'm going to need this for teaching now that I am well." The needles bit into my flesh anew.

Mother continued to amaze everyone, including me, with what appeared to be great health all during the next few months.

June of 1966 came, and the warm color of her skin began to fade and change ever so slightly to a grayed beige. I noticed. But I brushed it out of my mind. June, as it often is in California, was cool; but around the end of June and into the first week of July, the weather broke its pattern and blistered out into its finest example of dry heat.

On the Fourth of July our whole family gathered at my parents' home to have dinner together and to celebrate Independence Day. Their newly installed swimming pool was full of splashing water and noisy cousins and relatives having a great deal of fun.

In the midst of all the helloing and hugging and kissing going on, I did a double take at the sight of my mother's face. Instantly, it was as if the cactus punched thousands of holes in my mind, because I was sure she had not been cured, only given a remission. Mother had asked for fifteen years more, and she had thought she had it. I believed she had not heard the Lord clearly. I was sure he had answered her request by saying, *No, Marion, not fifteen years. Only six months.*

As I analyze that scene by the pool, I can now see that Mother did not have a spontaneous, gradual, or circumstantial healing, but a temporary healing. To me, her family, and her friends, it was a beautiful temporary healing that added six months of pain-free time to her life, six months that allowed her to serve God with a higher amount of devotion and love than anybody within a thousand-mile radius. I and others have praised God for giving her those six months of freedom from pain. It doesn't even matter that we did not understand what type of healing was done or that most of us were confused by it all. I'm just grateful to God that he gave her those months.

Mother did not have to tell me new lumps had formed like globules of cement in her remaining breast. I just knew, and I knew before she said, "Here, give me your hand. Feel this." She also didn't have to tell me that the pains in her chest were beginning to be unbearable. I could see her stiffen and hold her breath.

I sat on the edge of the pool that Fourth of July trying to keep my breaking heart under control. I faked small-talk type conversations with everyone. All in all, you could have said we had a wonderful family holiday, except for the brief moments when someone wasn't talking to me. Then I silently kicked and stirred circles in the pool water and wished it was I who had cancer and not she. I wondered what I would do the first time some well-meaning Christian said to me, "What do you mean, 'Marion is dying'? Why didn't God heal her? *Marion* said he did." What would I answer? I didn't even have any answers for me, much less for anyone else.

My mother called me out of my thoughts to come eat. I left the pool, sat down with everyone else, and found the food, no matter how hard I tried, would not go past my tongue. I felt like I had accidently fallen into a deep, dark, hidden pit. It was the pit of grief, and as I fell I tried to catch something, anything, to break my fall. But my fingers frantically clawed the sides of the pit, and nothing stopped my rapid descent. I fell and fell and fell, and kept on endlessly falling for days and days and days.

Mother had bargained with God, and he had given her some extra time in the form of a remission, but now it was over. I sensed time had run out and her death was drawing near.

My mother's bargaining with God was not abnormal or unusual behavior. Nor was it in any way wrong. It was a time of negotiating with God to come rescue her and give her more time here. I call this stage of the grief process our "basic battlefield bargaining." We cry out to God that if he gets us out of here (wherever that may be), or gets us through this nightmare (whatever that may be), and gives us more time, we'll serve him forever.

Actually, basic battlefield bargaining is hardly new. Jacob bargained all night with an angel for a blessing he desperately needed. Others have bargained with God for a miracle or simply for more time. I feel certain bargaining has transpired over and over again: in the woods around Gettysburg during the Civil War, in the trenches of World War I, in the foxholes of World War II, in the bitter cold of Korea, in the hills and swamps of Vietnam, and certainly right here at home where we thought we were safe and well protected from the enemy.

We must not look down our spiritual noses at those who crouch beneath the exploding shells of the war around them. We must not belittle them, criticize their lack of faith or demean them in any way. I guess my heart speaks out so forcefully because I'm doing my own basic battlefield bargaining with God at this moment in regard to my cancer.

Until God reveals his plan for us, we must sit patiently in his waiting room and put whatever amount of faith we have into trusting that he has his children's best interests at heart and *is* working things out for our good.

In music there is a term that describes my mother's bargaining: *rubato*. It describes the bargaining we all do with God to rescue and extend our lives here. According to my music dictionary, *rubato* means, "robbing or taking from the notes their strict time value by alternately hurrying and retarding for the purpose of expression."

Back in August of 1966, the *rubatoed* notes of the song of bargaining had ended for my mother. The six months were used up. No more could be accomplished. So she began her serious dying.

6

Regardless and Always

Her sun is gone down while it is yet day.
Jeremiah 15:9

I suppose there were brief moments during that raging hot July in 1966 when I stopped falling down that awful pit of grief and depression, but not many. In the middle of that month, I called Mother to ask her if she'd like to go shopping. She sounded tired and very ill, but her voice brightened upon hearing the word *shopping*, and she assured me she'd love to go.

I drove to Reseda and picked her up, then took her to her favorite shopping center, Topanga Plaza. Together we were doing what we loved to do. Both of us were like my friend Carolyn who, according to her husband, had the entire floor plan of every department store in the area committed to memory.

We were acting silly and feeling full of fun that day in Ohrbach's as we talked and walked from one department to another. I forgot about falling into pits. We laughed at some loosely crocheted bathing suits. They had large holes in them and were unlined, if you can picture that. In the hat department I sat down at a counter and tried on a large, floppy hat, struck what I hoped was a "movie star pose," and said, "Ta-Da!" My mother responded instantly with, "Oh, Julie Andrews, may I have your autograph?" Several clerks watched us and grew suspicious, which made it all the more hilarious. These moments are among my happiest frozen pictures of my mother. Every once in a while I thaw out these pictures and savor the joy.

After we'd examined everything on the first and second floors, we came back down the escalator and went over to the boys' department. Mother bought my son a shirt. As we waited at the cashier's stand, Mother, with a puzzled look on her face, said, "It's funny, but my memory seems to be getting worse. I know Rickie's thirteenth birthday is coming up on August 9, but I'm worried that I'll forget. Here, you take this shirt home and give it to him, okay?" The clerk gave her the change and we resumed our shopping. She bought both my sister, Marilyn, and my daughter, Laurie, a pair of sandals.

While we were looking at some blouses on the main floor I noticed that Mother had slowed her walking pace. She had also grown quiet. I looked at my watch and realized we'd been there almost two hours. I quickly suggested that we go home, but she said no and protested she was just fine. About then I remembered a pair of slippers I'd wanted to check out back in women's accessories, so I asked her to wait at the blouse counter and told her I'd be right back. I hurried down the aisle and found the slippers.

Just as the clerk asked me if I wanted any help something made me look back down the aisle at Mother. Ohrbach's was rather crowded with shoppers, but for that instant I had a clear view of my mother's head and shoulders in profile. She was leaning over a counter, standing quite still and looking down. Even from where I was I could see that she was very pale.

The clerk behind the counter held out a pair of slippers and said, "Are these the size you were looking for?" I may have answered her but I don't think so. All I do remember is that I shoved the slippers back into the clerk's hands and started running.

My mother is dying. We will never come to this place again. She is standing there saying good-bye to this store, as if it's her old friend. My God, help me to be strong. I pushed as fast as I could through the crowds until I reached her.

I slipped one arm around her and with my free hand took her packages. I could tell she was having a hard time breathing. "Let's go home, Mother," I said. She didn't move. I felt she wanted one more moment to say good-bye, so I waited. In a minute or so I said, "We must go now," and with her quiet "all right," we moved slowly toward the parking-lot entrance.

There were perhaps four hundred or so people in the store that day, but I'm sure none of them recognized the personal drama that was taking place. I left her at the outside entrance on the sidewalk, ran to get the car so she wouldn't have to walk, and drove back to pick her up. I doubt that anyone paid any attention to the tired, worn looking lady in the light blue dress. And I'm sure no one but me saw her turn, look back into the store, and ever so slightly nod her farewell to Ohrbach's. When she saw me, she left the entrance and settled herself into the car. Pretending I was her chauffeur, she gave a little smile and said, "Home, James!"

It was a memorable day for both of us. It was a day of my knowing she was dying. It was also a day of her knowing that not only was she going to die, but also we and all she loved would, in a sense, die and be taken from her. It was her time of grieving for her own death.

Within my head I heard grief's song transpose from a major key into the sad, lamenting strains of a minor key. It was a strange sound, haunting and even in its own way beautiful, but oh, so disturbing and filled with such deep sadness. To hear it was to cry softly.

Our sense of loss, loneliness, and grief was overwhelming. Both Mother and I experienced tremendous depression that day. Hers was in a different form from mine, but both of us were suffering from what Dr. Kübler-Ross calls "reactive depression." Later I saw my mother go into the other type of depression, which Dr. Kübler-Ross calls "preparatory"; and it was an awe-inspiring experience to watch her move through its dark tunnel and out the other side to acceptance.

The day after that shopping trip, during my prayer time, I came to the main issue in my life at that moment: coping with the terrible realization of my mother's oncoming death. Mentally I reviewed my full schedule of home and family duties as well as singing and speaking engagements. At that time I also had my own daily fifteen-minute radio show. Being a wife and mother were the top priorities on my goals list. The demanding schedule I was keeping wound me tight around its finger.

"Lord," I prayed, "*when* she dies, as I now know she will, please give me some advance notice when death is near. I want to spend her last weeks with her. I'll cancel all engagements, prerecord my radio program, freeze extra casseroles for my family, and do everything so I can be with her. I do not want to let my own fears about dying keep me from facing it or being with her. Please, Lord, I want no regrets after she's gone. I don't want to think I was so busy with my little world that I didn't take the time to wait with her while she died. So Lord, please tell me *when*."

My friend Marilu told me about one of her regrets. She had been notified of her nine-year-old son's death after he'd gone through a second surgery, and her very first thought had been, "Oh, I didn't give him a birthday party on his ninth birthday." It was a regret she carried for years. Eventually she worked through her natural, mother-type regret.

When I think about regrets, I remember an old man at Los Angeles International Airport who broke my heart over his regrets. We were both passengers waiting to board a flight to Hawaii. I was on my way overseas to do a speaking and singing tour for the United States Army Chaplains. The man was sitting near me when out of the corner of my eye I noticed he was silently crying. Just as I was about to ask him if I could help, a man on the other side of him did it for me.

The old man shook his head *no*, but he continued to cry. Then as he got a firmer grip on himself, he quietly began talking aloud to no one in particular. He began explaining why he was taking a trip to Hawaii. His wife had nagged him for thirty years about taking a Hawaiian vacation. Twenty years before, when they'd had the money for such a trip, she had nagged him even more. He recalled how he had firmly told her *no* and had given her his reasons. After all, he'd told her, he wasn't interested in Hawaii, and he couldn't see any point in going all that way and paying all that money just to see an island or two.

His voice filled with sadness, and then he looked at me and said, "Six months ago my wife got cancer and now, now she's gone." Though tears were streaming down his face, he made no move to dry them. "Just before she died, she made me promise I'd go and take that vacation in Hawaii for her. So here I am alone, going to Hawaii. . . . God, why didn't I take her when we had all the time . . . all those years?" The man on the other side of him put his arm around him and patted him.

I sat very still for a long time, thinking about the things I should do in my own life so I'd have no such sad trips to make. Studying the old man, I realized that while it was true he did have serious regrets, he was definitely in the process of working through them. He was keeping a promise he made to his dying wife, and I loved him for it! I prayed the trip to Hawaii would bring him some closure to the unfinished business of his regret.

At anyone's death there are bound to be some regrets, but I hoped that at least in my mother's case I wouldn't have any, or that they'd be held down to just a few. I also prayed that the regrets I might experience would not become a detriment to my own closure and healing after her death.

My unedited notes from that time were dated "Last week of July, 1966," under which I'd scribbled:

8:30 a.m.

I've tried not to think of her today, but it's hard not to. Even as I read the newspaper this morning something kept vaguely disturbing my reading. It was a dull, rather ordinary pain, but very persistent.

When I finished the (already) depressing newspaper, the pain got sharper. Then I remembered "she has cancer" and it returned with a vengeance.

Today, Mother goes to UCLA Medical Center. This time for the isotope (or something like that) treatments. Yesterday when I phoned her, her voice sounded so weak. I asked her if she was in any pain. She answered, "Oh, yes, the swelling in my chest is up. The fluid needs to be drained again. You might say this is a very bad day physically, but (her tone brightened as she continued), spiritually and mentally I couldn't be better!"

While it wasn't in my notes, I remember it was in that same phone conversation that Mother especially emphasized that I not go to the trouble of driving all the way over to the hospital to see her. She said the doctors had told her she would receive the chemotherapy and the "Bird" (inhalation) treatments and be home in about three days, probably by the weekend.

Since her stay was to be so brief I decided to honor her request and not make the trip to visit her. I called a florist and ordered a bouquet of flowers to be delivered to her room at UCLA Medical Center.

During the day I thought about her from time to time and prayed continuously, but I was neck-deep in all kinds of activities, prearranged schedules, etc. By late afternoon, however, my concern for her kept nagging at me, so I changed my mind. I knew I had to go see her.

When my husband got home from work I explained, "I don't know why, but can we go to UCLA? I think I need to see Mother." So after dinner we drove the hour or so across Los Angeles to the hospital.

At first glance, the University of California's Los Angeles Medical Center looks as picture-perfect as any other large, active, busy hospital. It's engraved on my memory. We parked and walked up through the emergency entrance, where the business of living and dying was briskly taking place. The halls were painted the traditional, nondescript hospital green, and the medicinal smells of Lysol, Clorox, and rubbing alcohol almost gagged me—just two of the reasons why I'm never entirely at ease in hospitals. In that area of the hospital, however, it wasn't as much the walls and aroma that got to me as it was the rush and press of so many people.

Doctors were talking as they gathered in tight little circles, looking (to me) far too young to be making so many responsible life-and-death decisions. Nurses stood or sat as they wrote out their endless reports, registering either boredom or fatigue on their faces. Technicians sauntered down the halls with trays of blood-test samples as casually as if they were carrying tubes of tomato juice. The cleaning staff was valiantly trying to work their floor-wash equipment in and around gurneys, clustered doctors, patients, and distraught families.

As we neared the elevator a little girl being carried by her mother vomited over her mother's shoulder; the remains of her lunch splashed down in front of me onto the just-washed, shiny floor. A cleaning man behind me uttered a sigh and said something about it being the third time he'd cleaned that floor today. He moved his pail back toward the mess.

We pushed the third-floor button and stepped into the elevator. Its quiet motor noise came as a few seconds of welcome relief. We stepped off the elevator onto the third floor, and I didn't have to ask which room was Marion Miller's. I had no trouble finding my mother's room, even though it was down at the end of a long corridor. It took the grand prize for noise. I remember being guided down that hall by the sound of my mother's laughter. "It was silly of me to make this long trip over here for nothing," I thought. Mother sounded so good; so normal; so absolutely fine.

She was the only person I saw when I entered the room. Sitting cross-legged on the middle of her bed, she was reading aloud some cards and letters she'd received. There she sat, in a new and darling robe, looking fresh as a daisy. She let out a whoop of joy when she saw us and said, "What in the world are you two doing here?" For the second time in two minutes, I wondered that myself. She'd never looked better. Yet I knew from talking with her the day before that she'd been having a difficult time breathing and that the pain had been substantial. Still, she looked marvelous.

We called our hellos to my dad and were introduced to Mother's roommate in the bed across the room. After some polite chitchat, I went over and stood at the foot of Mother's bed. She was pointing out my bouquet of flowers on the nightstand and was thanking us. I stood there looking at what had to be the poorest excuse for an expensive florist arrangement I'd ever seen and was thinking, *Next time I'll send candy.* But Mother seemed to think the flowers were lovely and was saying so when I heard it the first time. Clearly, a voice from somewhere in my head said, *She is dying now.*

My mother thought my outburst of "Ha!" was in response to her statements about the flowers; actually, it bounced out of me because I couldn't believe the words I thought I'd heard. I wasn't able to fit the message with the very healthy visual image Mother presented.

I know now that I took one giant step backward into denial. I told myself she might die, but certainly it would not be now. Then I heard the words again. *She is dying now.* I looked around, wondering if anyone else had heard it.

A few minutes later, I called my father aside and said, "Dad, have the doctors said *anything* to you about Mother's, ah . . . condition?"

"Oh, yes," he was cheerfully matter-of-fact. "They think she's doing just fine, and they say she'll be home in two days."

Just then a couple of doctors came in. It was obvious that they were eager to say hello to Mother. Loudly and with much kidding they renewed their previously established friendship with her.

She is dying. Now. The third time I heard it, I said in my heart, "Lord, look at her. Look at the doctors, look at my father. *They* think she's just fine. Am I the only one who knows?"

You asked me to tell you when she would die. I am telling you. It's time. She is dying now. The quiet answer was loud enough for me to hear even above the noisy din of conversation in Mother's room.

As the doctors left, I followed them out into the hall. "Doctor," I called to one of them, then continued, "I'm Mrs. Miller's daughter. I'm a big girl and have had my share of tragic losses. I do not want to be coddled or spared anything relative to my mother's condition. So please tell me what her prognosis is." Both doctors looked at me and then at each other in amazement. In a tone that suggested they were shocked I'd even questioned her prognosis, they insisted, "She's just fine. This is a routine trip for her. You don't have to worry. She'll be out of here by Friday."

I don't think so, I said to myself; and very puzzled, I walked back to Mother's room. While I had been gone, the inhalation therapist had set up the Bird equipment and had begun the treatment for Mother.

I was still thinking about the overwhelming words the Lord had so clearly put into my mind, and my face must have reflected the seriousness of the message. My mother mistook my worried expression, so she took off her oxygen mask and said, "Oh, honey, don't let this bother you. It just helps me breathe, and after I've had this treatment I feel so much better." I was still deeply perplexed by what I had heard that night.

We stayed for a little longer, then I hugged her and said my good-byes. As I left her bedside and started down the hall toward the elevators, the green-painted hall began to spin and swirl around me. I reached out and grabbed the railing mounted on the wall. My husband said quietly, "I think you better prepare yourself. I don't think your mother is ever going to leave here alive."

His words seemed to restore my sanity. I thanked the Lord that someone else felt she was dying. I started crying in the elevator and had to lean up against the chain-link fence in the parking lot with uncontrollable sobbing. For the next three days I couldn't stop crying. My own grieving process was in full swing.

At home the next day, I received a long letter from Mother. She had written it about an hour before she'd gone to the hospital. It was the very last letter she was to write. It was typical of her to write a just-in-case letter to tell me of her love— just in case something prevented her from doing so in person.

Evidently, on the day she was to go to UCLA she'd felt better than she had in a long time, so she backtracked from acceptance down into the bargaining stage. At one point in her letter she wrote:

Today I go to UCLA again. I'm sure of the promise and love of God and know He will completely heal me. He said it was finished and by His stripes I am healed. He promises *seventy years and by reason of strength even eighty—I think I, as a Christian who has the life of Christ within her, can claim health.*

I do not ask in my own merits—but as a child of God redeemed—I ask in Jesus' name! God does not heal because I deserve it—but because Jesus paid for it and redeemed me. Praise God.

I wished I could believe and accept that God would heal her. I wished I had her assurance and confidence. But I simply didn't. Yet, the last lines of her letter told me that God was preparing her not for healing, but for death, in spite of what she'd written about her guaranteed healing from God.

She had written the letter in her typical breezy style, and her beautiful penmanship reflected a bit of hurry. Then, just before she signed her name at the bottom of the page, it looked to me as if she stopped, even if briefly, and wrote very clearly, deliberately, and legibly her last but most important message to me. She wrote with a steady and unhurried hand, probably so I wouldn't miss her meaning:

It's almost noon. I must close and get ready to go at 1:00 p.m. So much love and prayer to you all my dear children.

Keep faith with God—regardless and always.

Lovingly your
Mother

Also, one of your ardent fans!

Mom

My eyes went back to her one-liner about keeping the faith with God—regardless and always. This was her written farewell. *Regardless*—of what would or could happen, I was to keep faith with God. *And always*, forever, I was to keep faith with God until we'd meet again. These were the words of the legacy she left me on paper, my last just-in-case letter.

To everyone's surprise but mine, Mother didn't come home that weekend. Nobody but me seemed to be upset. The doctors smiled and assured me that she would stay over the weekend but would certainly be home by the following Wednesday. When Wednesday rolled around, everyone at the hospital got very quiet, and they stopped predicting release dates.

Mother was in the hospital less than a week by the time I checked my schedules, canceled engagements, and made my family comfortable so I could stay with her at UCLA. I was totally unprepared for what I saw when I walked into her room. In the brief days since I'd last seen her, Mother had gone from bright-eyed-and-bushy-tailed enthusiasm to a flat-on-her-back struggle to breathe, even with an oxygen mask.

Mother's denial had stamped itself into anger. Anger had burned out into bargaining. Bargaining had dissipated itself into depression and grief. I wondered when grief would begin to lift into a quiet and peaceful acceptance. But I knew for sure her dying process had begun.

While I visited her that day she asked me to help her sit up. So I cranked the bed up, and she removed the oxygen mask and laid it beside her. That was the moment she told me that she had taught me how a Christian should *live* for my thirty-four years and that now she was going to show me how a Christian *dies*. Typical of her, she was dramatic, spiritual, and yet completely practical. Immediately after her poignantly beautiful words, she reached over to her nightstand, slid open a drawer, and brought out a yellow legal pad of paper. Handing me the pad and a new ball-point pen, she said, "Here, I want you to take notes."

You're kidding, I thought. *She wants me to take notes on my own mother's dying? Impossible.* I looked down at the pad she'd just handed me and read the words *Book Titles* at the top of the page. Under that she had written what appeared to be nine titles for women's books.

She watched my face as I read them, and when she saw my head shaking in disbelief she said, "Oh, those are just some titles you might want to write a book about. I was lying here thinking about the senior editor at Zondervan Publishing House who asked you to write, and I jotted down some ideas for titles. You write the books, Joyce-Honey, I'll do the hard part." She laughed at her little joke. I was still back on "take notes."

Oh, Dr. Elisabeth Kübler-Ross, you were so right when you said we have so much to learn from the dying. Very few of us are willing to pick up the notebooks and pens, to be students and take notes, because tuition feels too costly. Standing by, leaning on, and lying on a deathbed beside our teacher seems an endless, bittersweet assignment. In dealing with the dying, poignant conversation and painful fatigue seem to blend together. They fill up every space and crevice in us until finally they ooze out all our pores, and we've had enough; we don't want to learn. But, oh, the messages and lessons of the dying.

While Mother didn't know exactly how long she'd have, she must have sensed it would be brief. Every day of her last seven weeks I felt like I was cramming for some kind of crucial final exam.

I know now that the notebook pad was given to me for a twofold purpose. She knew me well enough to know that if I had something creative to do with my time while I waited with her, she could go on teaching me the last lessons of her life. The pad of paper was as much for her as it was for me. She mentioned a number of times how concerned she was about my speaking schedule. "What have you done? *Canceled* them?" It was a preposterous thought to her. When I told her that I had indeed changed my whole schedule, her mind instantly began to devise a plan to keep me busy. (Did she know about *this* book and how heavily I'd rely on those notes of mine? I think so!)

Secondly, she was projecting beyond the moment of her death. I'm sure Mother wanted to make certain that I'd work through and past my grief. Wisdom told her that one of the best ways for me to do that was to physically pick up a pen and write on a project: hence, the book titles. The titles were designed to force me to think about writing so that my self-centered preoccupation with grief would ease and phase out. Then I'd be able to move into a creative direction. I think she knew that actually writing books would require a supreme amount of effort and concentration; and she didn't want to think of me sitting around in apathy, rotting away with each new day. So she gave me a vision, yes, even projects to do— *after.*

A few years after my mother's death, I attended the funeral of Mrs. Harms, a dear friend of mine and of my mother. I walked up to her casket to tell her good-bye. She looked lovely. She was the mother of my friend Ruth Harms Caulkin and had been present at the birthday luncheon Ruth had given for my mother and me. I bent over her casket and mentioned that I loved her hair. It looked beautiful and was fixed the way she would have wanted it. Then I added, "For goodness sake, Mom Harms, don't forget to tell my mother I *wrote* all those books she told me to!" My mother had been so right in knowing I'd need a project.

Nothing my mother taught was more of an object lesson than the familiar pink cardboard box she gave me. She had come to the hospital to stay only three days. Her little overnight bag had held some nighties, a robe, and the little pink box.

"Here, Joyce-Honey," she said one day, "take my pink box. I won't be needing it anymore." I opened the box, intending to show her she'd be sorry if I took it home, but I shut it and put it by my purse after I'd looked inside. All her personal items—curlers, hairbrush and comb, lipstick, powder, cleansing cream, lotion, toothpaste—all those things were being given to me. It was another way she'd come up with to help me accept the inevitability of her death. She had moved into acceptance and wanted, without words, to help me move graciously into it, too.

"Some of those cosmetics are excellent products. They're expensive and very good. You use them in good health, honey!" (I choked on that one.) All these years later, I still have one of the beauty aids from that little pink box, and it reminds me of a mother who gracefully accepted her death and assisted me in my acceptance.

A doctor once told me he could always tell when a woman patient was getting well because she'd begin combing her hair, or she'd put on a little lipstick, especially if it were almost time for visiting hours. He told me he always watched for these signs to check his patient's progress toward recovery. My mother's case was the opposite story. When she accepted dying, she knew she would no longer need combs, brushes, or cosmetics, so she made a big deal of giving them to me.

The day after she gave them to me, my friend Eleanor came to visit Mother. When Eleanor left, my mother asked in a confidential whisper, "How did Eleanor think I looked?" I asked her what she meant. "Well, honey, I mean I've changed [she pointed to her face]. Did Eleanor notice it or say anything about it?"

Out in the hall before she had left the hospital, Eleanor had in fact mentioned the enormous physical changes she'd seen. The last time she'd seen Mother was at the memorable birthday luncheon she and Ruth had given for us when Mother, in her late fifties, had suddenly begun to enjoy a remission. Now she looked like a woman of eighty years or more.

It struck me for the first time how much the dying are aware of the physical changes occurring in them. And how they fear that if they become too ugly or too disfigured, they will be unlovable and untouchable. Even though Mother had not seen herself in a mirror, she knew she had lost much weight and had guessed the truth. She knew she was nothing more than tightly drawn gray skin over bones, and that her short hair hung limp and lifeless around her face.

I tried assuring her. "Mother, Eleanor knows you are very sick, and she understood about your hair. It didn't bother her." Mother looked relieved.

"Oh, I'm glad; I must look a mess."

To try to lighten her fears and cheer her I said, "That's right. As a matter of fact, you actually look crummy. But I love every crummy thing about you." A tiny smile played across her mouth, and she hit the ball right back into my court with, "You don't look so hot yourself. Have you thought of leaving here and going home to wash your hair?"

That was the only time we talked about appearances, but from then on I made a special point of lightly brushing her hair and reassuring her she looked much better after I'd used my magic touch. Both of us knew I was at a complete loss in the hair-combing department, and we also knew our conversation was a game. But it seemed to ease her fears and help her realize we were not about to stop loving her just because she was changing physically.

One morning, while my father was still generally optimistic about my mother's condition, I realized that my brother, Cliff, should come home from Vietnam to visit Mother one last time. My dad was deep into denial, however, and said he didn't think Mother's illness was serious enough to send for Cliff. I remember being terribly angry with him. I decided to take matters into my own hands. I went back to the hospital and suggested, "Mother, you are so sick. Don't you think we ought to get Cliff out of Vietnam and home? Wouldn't you like to see him?" She opened her eyes very wide and breathed out the words, "Oh, yes!" My dad meekly said "Fine" and called the Red Cross. Less than eighteen hours later my brother, right out of the mine-infested jungles of Vietnam, went to see Mother.

My notes on my pad of paper read rather cryptically,

Isotope couldn't be used. They inserted a drainage tube today and Cliff flew home from Vietnam.

There was much more to it, however, than my notes described. I left the hospital to spend a couple of hours at home and just missed seeing Cliff. He had taken one look at Mother and immediately phoned me at home.

"What's going on?" he almost yelled. "How come nobody told me she was terminal? She's *dying*, Joyce." He was a marine corpsman and had been dealing with the wounded and dying on Vietnam battlefields day in and day out for months. Death was part of his regular daily routine, and he recognized it when he saw it. He went on to tell me that not one of Dad's letters had said anything remotely serious about Mother. Why hadn't Dad leveled with him? He wanted an explanation.

As I have said, I wish I'd known more about denial. I wish I'd been familiar with denial's shapes, attitudes, words, and actions. I think I could have explained it so much better to myself and to Cliff that day. Instead, I told him how angry I was with Dad. I related to him the many times I'd gotten off the elevator on UCLA's terminal patient third floor and started toward the left corridor only to hear someone whistling, humming, or singing, and happily jingle-jangling his keys—and I'd known it was our father. The meeting and conversation there by the nurses' station was always the same.

"Hi, dearie," he'd say cheerfully.

"Hi, Dad. How's Mother right now?" Then every bone in my body would tense and scream in unison, *please, please* don't tell me she's "just fine."

"Why, she's just fine," he'd answer. Cliff listened to this story in silence. I could feel his anger. When we said goodbye, I was left with a hollow feeling that nothing had been resolved.

I remember that one day I could hold in my feelings no longer. "Dad, how can you say that? She's lost weight, she's not able to sit up anymore. She's on oxygen all the time. Her

skin is gray. Mother's dying and she knows it! She wants to
go home to heaven."

"Oh, now, Joyce." He put his arms around my stiffening
shoulders, patted me, and said, "Why, all she needs is some
of Grandma Uzon's Hungarian chicken soup."

Terrific, I thought. *What all these brilliant doctors heading
up cancer-research teams don't know is that Hungarian chicken
soup is the answer!* Dad went off down the hall, whistling and
doing his thing with the keys. (I think he went to Grandma's
to get some soup.)

A nurse came out of a room, recognized me, and asked,
"Could I have a minute with you, Mrs. Landorf?" Then very
secretively she said, "Ah . . . your father is a minister, right?"

"Right," I said.

"Well, that makes it even harder to understand."

"Harder to understand what?" I asked.

"Well, he's had people in his congregation die and surely
he knows about terminally ill patients . . . ah . . . doesn't he
know your mother is terminal?"

I explained that I had practically screamed that news at
him, but he wouldn't or couldn't hear me.

By now Mother had been in the hospital almost five weeks.
The doctors were more than perplexed. My notes are short
but graphic here.

Doctor C. said, "Prognosis is poor. Very poor. I don't
know how she can get any sicker than she is and still live."
Dad keeps on talking to us as if she has a chest cold. I don't
know how I can stand the strain of his attitude. He is very
mad at Cliff because Cliff told him the Lord might take
Mother home very soon.

Dad listened to Doctor C., nodded his head like he understood the words, but walked away without hearing a thing.

Mother is now on an IV of dextrose and is being catheterized. *All that's left of her is her beautiful brown eyes. Cancer has taken everything else.*

Two days later, my notes are supershort

Now he says all she needs is vitamins!

Later that day, Dad bought Mother a new refrigerator. "Why?" I wearily asked, knowing the answer before he spoke.

"Why, our old fridge is on the fritz and when she gets home she'll just love this new one."

Then, as he was going down the hall he said something like, "I'm thinking about going to the travel agency. You know your mother always wanted to go to Hawaii . . ."

I think *I* came close to being terminal in that instant, or maybe I felt like I was going stark, raving insane. I never quite knew which.

I left the UCLA Medical Center to go home for a few hours of rest only to have the worst, and to date only, argument with my then fourteen-year-old sister, Marilyn.

She was standing in Laurie's bedroom, and she looked so darling. There is twenty years' difference in our ages, and Marilyn's only a year and a half older than my son, Rick. I've always loved her as one of my own rather than as a sister. Our conversation started gently enough with her question: "Will Mother get better?"

Most experts feel children should have their questions on death and sex answered in the same manner. We should be truthful but answer only the child's immediate question. We should not run ahead of him or her by answering unasked questions that are too heavy for the child to carry.

I suspected that since my father was so deep in denial, I was the logical person to answer my sister's painful question about death; but I remember standing there, emotionally and physically exhausted, asking "Why me?" and wondering where I'd dredge up the strength to handle this confrontation.

I took a deep breath, prayed that God would give me wisdom, and quietly began. "Well, Marilyn, honey, if Mother had been in a car accident with both legs broken, ribs cracked, and all wrapped up in casts and bandages, and you asked if she'd get better, I'd say, 'Yes, in time.' In fact, I could even assure you that from what we knew of her injuries, her recovery wouldn't take too long. But today when I looked at all the signposts and symptoms Mother shows, lying there with advanced breast and now lung cancer, I have to tell you, 'No, honey, she is going to die.'"

Marilyn's dark brown eyes were blazing with anger, and she snapped, "She's not going to die. She's going to get well. God promised me Mother would get well." I felt terribly frustrated and knew I'd failed with her. I was tired and mad at my father's refusal to see what was happening; and now to face the same denial from my sister broke all the pins loose on my emotions. I almost screamed at her, "*Mother is dying.*"

"No, she's not," Marilyn cried and insisted. "Besides, how can you be so sure?"

"I just told you. By the signs," I said sternly.

"But God promised me he'd make her well. He promised. He promised!" she countered.

I went out in the hall, determined to leave her alone with her denial, but I couldn't do that to her. So I asked God to somehow give me the right words for this delicate moment. I knew I had to bring this painful issue to a truthful conclusion. To the Lord I uttered a cry for help and went back into the bedroom.

"Marilyn, do you remember when my baby David was born?"

She turned her face to me. "Yes," she nodded her head.

"Well, I want to tell you something I've never told anyone else. I only had one fleeting look at David, but when I saw him, my *only* prayer was, 'Oh, Lord—make him well.' And you know what, Marilyn, honey, God answered my prayer by healing David, though not *exactly* the way I hoped he would. I believed God had promised me that David would be well. I had no way of knowing that God meant to heal David in *heaven*—not here on earth! Marilyn, could it be possible that when God promised you Mother would be well, he meant in heaven and not in Reseda, California?"

I'm sure she was still fiercely angry with me, but she was tired and hurt by all the conflicts surrounding Mother. So I left her lying on Laurie's bed, covered with the blankets of her newly found grief. I left her alone so she could begin to face the unalterable fact that Mother was not "holding her own and resting," as Dad had continually told everyone, but was in all probability dying.

My time with Marilyn that day was used of God, but my repeated tries with my father's denial gained no such success! My anger toward Dad's denial was catching hold of me because not only was I unable to understand it, but also I was by this time terribly sick of the dying process. I was also angry at God for letting time drag my mother in and out of one agonizing day after another.

One day at the hospital, I realized out of the blue that my much-beloved mother wasn't getting any cards, flowers, or even phone calls from the many women who dearly loved her. I also got to wondering where in the world were all the wonderful people from my father's church. None of them had visited Mother, and hardly any had sent flowers or other messages. It wasn't like them to be aloof. They were warm, giving people who loved the pastor's wife, Marion.

A couple of mornings later I left the hospital to go home for a few hours. About noon I thought I'd better call Mother's room. Maybe a nurse, if one was by her bedside, could give me a quick progress report. The phone was answered instantly in a voice that sounded very familiar but wasn't my mother's or a nurse's.

"Dottie? Dottie, is that you? This is Joyce," I said. There was a long silence on the other end, but I knew it was Dottie, a friend and one of the women from Dad's church. Finally, she whispered into the phone, "Joyce, this is awful—your mother is dying."

"Yes, I know," I answered wearily, wondering aloud what had brought her to my mother's room. Dottie explained, "Last night I was praying and having devotions, and the Lord said, *Go see Marion.*" Then she'd had this rather bizarre argument with the Lord about my dad having told the congregation that there was nothing seriously wrong. Dad had assured them that all Marion needed was rest and had requested that they not visit her, as they might tire her. Dottie had called my sister, and Marilyn had said, "Mother's holding her own."

"But," Dottie continued, "this morning the Lord really impressed upon me the feeling I should go see Marion, so I came. I'm sorry if I wasn't supposed to, but Joyce . . . she's dying."

I told her that my Dad was unable to face the fact that my mother was dying, and that I was relieved that she knew. I asked her to go back to the church and tell the people that Mother didn't have too long. I also requested that she ask them to pray that Mother's death would be soon, because she was in tremendous pain and was having trouble breathing.

I didn't go back to the hospital that day as I'd planned. I suspect I was very depressed about Dad's not admitting to himself, or to anyone, the reality of Mother's condition. Late that night, when I was at my lowest point, the phone rang, and it was Dad calling from the hospital. His message was one unbelievable line: "Mother's sinking fast. Come quickly."

Leaving my husband with our children, I drove at neck-breaking speeds toward the hospital. I thought, *We've come from "All she needs is soup and vitamins" to "She's sinking fast."* Relieved, I thought, *Finally, Dad's facing the situation as it really is.*

Mother had suffered a slight heart attack. Her heart was still fibrillating quite a bit, even by the time I got there. My father was a picture of peace, but for once he did not tell me, "She's just fine." He told me how he had sung to her. (She must have loved that. My dad had a beautiful voice, and thirty-five years earlier, his voice and his violin playing had been the first things that had made Mother fall in love with him.) In the hospital he had sung, "Good-bye, Our God Is Watching O'er You," among other favorites of hers.

All through the night we sat with her; and then my dad, for the first time facing the reality of her death, prayed a beautiful prayer. My notes only recall his last words. He attempted to bargain with God, asking,

Let her see the morning light, if it be thy will . . . and we shall praise thee forever. Amen.

By dawn her heartbeat had become fairly stable, her color was no longer ashen gray, and it seemed that the crisis had passed. With the passing of that crisis, however, passed my dad's acceptance. He went right back into his whistling, key-jangling denial. By late that afternoon he was telling my sister that Mother had passed the crisis, and now she would be well. I don't remember what I said, and for sure I didn't take notes, but I do remember standing outside Mother's room in the hall and telling him in several hundred different ways that what he'd just told Marilyn was *not true.*

I begged him to snap out of his irrational behavior. I treated him like he was a spoiled child stamping his foot for candy. I put him down very hard that day and angrily told him off as I'd never had the courage to do before. After I had spent all my anger on him, he very quietly walked over to where Marilyn was standing. He put one arm around her shoulders, and facing me, made a stunning announcement. "I only have *one* daughter," he said clearly.

I deserved the remark. I wish I'd known about the side effects of denial, and I wish I'd stood aside to let Dad's denial run its course. I couldn't get it through my head that denial was something he couldn't help or control.

I wish, too, I had had some magic way, some type of video

preview, that would have made it possible for me to see him as he would be two weeks after my mother's death. I would have known the exact moment his denial was dropped for good.

I was to learn months later that Dad went up to northern California after Mother's funeral to spend a few days with old friends. On the first night he was there he couldn't sleep, so he got up, dressed, and took a walk through walnut groves. As he was walking down one of the moonlit lanes between the trees, he suddenly remembered something interesting that had happened on the trip up there that day. Chuckling, he stopped and said out loud, "Oh, I must remember to tell Marion about that when I get home." And then for the first heart-piercing time, he realized she was not at home. She would never be at home. She was gone. Dad told me how he had crumpled down beside one of those old walnut trees, stayed there, and cried out his grief until dawn.

In retrospect, I see I could have given him so much more grace, and I could have—would have—been infinitely more patient with him. It still saddens me that my ignorance caused so much unnecessary friction between us.

My notebook from a few days later reads:

Doctor C. told me, "Medically speaking, your mother should have died during that last crisis."

Doctor F. told Cliff, "She doesn't have months. Maybe weeks, but personally, I think only days."

The Red Cross extended Cliff's leave.

Last night both Cliff and I were there. Mother's fluid must have been building rapidly because she started to become irrational. To calm her I asked her if I could read to her. She insisted we both go home. Her breathing was very labored. Before we left she must have been in great pain (or perhaps she's tired of waiting, too) because she pulled me down close to her mouth and said, "Joyce, pray. Pray."

On the elevator I looked over at Cliff and asked rhetorically, "How much longer can this continue?" He just shrugged his shoulders.

We are all so tired.

The next day as I entered Mother's room I met the hospital's chaplain. I'd missed him on his other visits to Mother, but his face lit up when I introduced myself.

"So you're Marion Miller's *Joyce*! Oh, she's talked of you and your work—your singing and your radio program. I feel like I know you!" Immediately after we talked I picked up my pad so I'd have a sentence of his conversation with me written down. My notes read:

Chaplain H.: "I go to see your mother quite often to give her a little lift, but each time I come away with the biggest lift for myself. You know, Joyce, your mother is not afraid to die. The death of a Christian like your mother is so beautiful. Just think, try to picture, your mother and her joy on entering heaven. Think, too, on all the joy they will have in welcoming her. I imagine she won't be there very long before someone says, 'Marion, I'm here because of you!'"

My dear chaplain, you were a beautiful ray of hope that afternoon, and you momentarily returned my sanity to me after all those debilitating and bewildering weeks. I don't know where you are right know, but knowing that God does, I've asked him to bless your life in a special way right this minute. I will always be grateful to you.

My friend and author Ruth Harms Caulkin lost both her father and mother within a few short months of each other, and she penned:

> Lord,
> If like a fragile flower
> Torn petal by petal
> My heart must continue to tear,
> Let there be fragrance.

In those awful, seemingly endless weeks of waiting, I felt sure that there would be no fragrance of any kind, and certainly no worthwhile aroma would permeate the air around me. I was wrong.

Neither the doctors nor I knew it then, but Mother had one more week to endure, one more week of waiting, watching, and learning for us, and seven more days—168 hours—of excruciating pain. It was like a rerun of a TV show segment titled, "The Week That Was!"

The fragrance that was crushed out of that wild, marvelous week still, so many years later, swirls around me, filling my heart and lungs with its pungent and savory potpourri of memories. I have come to know that the fragrance of Mother's life and death is strong enough to last, regardless and always . . . regardless and always.

7
Death and the Sound of Music

The wicked is overthrown by this mischief-making,
but the righteous, while dying, has confidence.
Proverbs 14:32 MLB

Andraé Crouch's contagious song "I Got Confidence"
was probably not composed to sing around the beds of the
dying, but as the above quote from Proverbs tells us, the
righteous, while dying, have confidence. So I can hardly think
of a better song to sing! Even now, as I work on this newest
edition of *Mourning Song*, I am reminded of the passage from
Proverbs.

Less than a month ago, a beautiful woman in our church,
Irene Cochran, in her eighties, was suffering from both breast
and lung cancer. Our current pastor, Dr. Gerald Mann, inter-
viewed her one Sunday morning in all three worhip services
of Riverbend Baptist Church in Austin, Texas. I was too ill
from my chemo treatments to attend, but I have a tape of
Irene's conversation with our pastor that morning.

They talked of her appointment with death, or as Dr. Mann
called it, the "ultimate healing." Then, in a voice filled with

a serene confidence, Irene said, "When we think about dying, often we think about, you know, putting our body in that hole in the ground. Well, when you really face it, you don't think of that. You think about going to be with Jesus, and this picture diminishes—"

Dr. Mann interjected here, "You don't think of what you're leaving—you think of where you're going." And Irene confirmed his words with a hearty "That's right!" One week later, almost to the exact hour of that interview, Irene Cochran went confidently home to be with Jesus.

Another drama showing the confidence given the righteous was played out before me in my father's dying days in the late '80s. My husband Francis and I watched Dad come out of the lethargy of dying and ended up singing several songs with him. What surprised us most was that during the time we were singing, his marvelous voice seemed to come alive and throb with strength and beauty. A few days later, he was with the Lord he'd loved and served almost all his life. He left with great confidence as to who he was (a child of God) and where he was going (heaven).

It was way back in September of 1966, the last week of my mother's life, that I first heard and distinctly felt that God-given confidence about dying, although I doubt that at the time I recognized it as such. Even though few of us understand the ways and workings of God, my mother showed great insight as she spent her last week serenely alive. I witnessed her great beauty, which was the loveliness of God-given confidence in the face of dying. Its dignity was apparent not just to me but to all who saw her.

That week Mother was filled with lessons she wanted to leave with me. She did not know the exact time of death, but she could hear the rustle of the death angel's wings and knew it would be soon. She would doze, as the dying usually do, and then suddenly, remembering the urgency of the moment, she would say something important to me and then drop off to sleep. The dying are like babies, who need large amounts of sleep. I liked watching the peaceful sleep which eased her, for a few moments now and then, out from the intensity of her pain.

My grandmother and my Aunt Grace had been vacationing in the East, but as soon as they reached home and heard about Mother they hurried over to the hospital. When they had left on vacation my mother had been in fairly good health, but now they saw a very different Marion—weak, weighing about eighty pounds, and dying.

Just as they were visiting her, my mother began to have a slight heart attack. The doctors, nurses, and staff flew into the room and hurriedly tried to usher out Mother's relatives. I say *tried,* because they didn't succeed until my grandmother had had her say.

Grandma took one good look at all the equipment, IV bottles, and activity surrounding my mother, and angrily, in her broken Hungarian-English, she startled the nearest doctor with, "Vy you do this? You stop. You let her go. You not keep her here. She ready to see God." My aunt hustled Grandma out the door before she could throttle the young doctor. My grandmother's confidence in God's plan was strong and steady. She thought it was terrible to prolong a life like Marion's and to keep her here, holding her back from going to heaven.

A little later one of the hospital attendants took my Aunt Grace aside and asked her who the older lady was. My aunt explained it was Marion's mother.

"Oh, dear!" the attendant said adamantly. "It's a mistake to have such an elderly lady here. Does she know of her daughter's condition? Does she know that she's terminal?" she asked.

"Yes," my aunt assured her.

"Then you should take her home. It's too hard on the aged to see their children die. Take her home."

My aunt stood her ground and wisely answered, "No. I'm not taking her home until she's ready to leave. It's not wrong that she's here. You don't know her. But I do, and I can tell you one thing: she's a praying mother. If my sister died and I hadn't let Mother see her, Mother would spend the rest of her life saying to me, 'You didn't tell me about Marion, so I didn't pray. How could you do that to me? Maybe God would have spared her life.' This way," my aunt continued, "our mother has been told, she's seen Marion, she's prayed, and now she's left it up to God."

"I see," murmured the attendant. But I'm not sure she did. My grandmother had taken stock of the whole hospital scene, and knowing God was about to take her daughter, accepted her daughter's death without reservations. She had prayed, and now it was up to God. How dare anyone interfere with God, she wanted to know. Not only the righteous while dying have confidence, but the righteous who stand by have a goodly share of it too!

My mother survived the crisis of that day and by the next morning was back to dozing, sleeping, and occasionally talking. The nurse's aide who brought the breakfast tray broke into a wide grin when she saw Mother.

"Hello, Mrs. Miller. How are you today?" Without waiting for a reply she continued, "Are you going to be a good girl today and eat your breakfast?"

Mother smiled and said, "I'm not really hungry, but for you, I'll try."

The attendant stopped her well-developed routine, reached over the bedrail, and gently touched Mother's face. It was the gesture of a caring person, and its effect was not lost on Mother. I loved watching the scene because the woman's touch shared that unspoken feeling of caring. Mother smiled and responded with, "Thank you. I hope you have a wonderful day today."

The woman glanced up at me, and I could see she was deeply touched. Here was a dying patient advising *her* to have a good day. She positioned the breakfast tray and left, her eyes brimming with tears.

I put a spoonful of oatmeal to Mother's mouth, but after one small bite she said, "Please, no more. It sticks right here in my throat and it won't go down."

I quit trying to feed her and asked if I could read to her instead. She smiled and nodded toward her nightstand where a new translation of the New Testament was lying. She didn't ask for any specific scriptures, so I flipped the Bible open and began reading Colossians 2:1. Somewhere about the seventh verse, I realized I was not speaking alone.

"Mother, have you memorized this entire chapter?" She'd not missed a word with me.

"Oh, yes," she said. "This is an exciting chapter!"

"But it's a brand-new translation. It's only been published a few months, and you already know it?" I was stunned and marveled again at the agility of her mind. We finished the chapter together. I read, she recited. Her sense of wonder at the promises of God was just as great as her sensitivity to the hospital attendant.

If the dying do not have that sense of wonder, then death becomes something fearfully horrible. And I believe that without God's positive reinforcement of love, dying becomes a dark journey down a long tunnel that ends in a brick wall. This was to be the subject of my first lesson.

Later that day, Mother opened her eyes and, finding me there, said, "You know, Joyce Honey, there are worse things to die of than this [she patted her chest]." From all the excruciating suffering I'd seen her go through with breast and lung cancer, I wasn't too sure I agreed with her. But I asked anyway, "Like what?"

"Well," she answered thoughtfully, "you know, you could die of loneliness, like the kind the newly divorced suffer from, or worse yet—you could die alone, without God." She settled down deeply into her pillow. "Yes," she sighed, "that would be the *worst* death possible."

Our conversation was interrupted by a short visit from Aunt Grace. As she and Mother talked, I prepared to rub

Mother down with some lotion, but Aunt Grace took the bottle from me and gently began massaging the lotion into my mother's cracked and drying hands. Not many minutes after Aunt Grace had gone, Mother said, "Joyce-Honey—"

"Yes, Mother?"

"Why was Grace so tender to me?"

"She knows you don't have long, Mother." There was a long silence and finally:

"Joyce?"

"Yes?"

"Promise me something?"

"I promise. What do you want?"

"I want you to promise me, honey, that you'll never stop praying for her. You know she needs the Lord."

"Yes, I know. I promise, Mother."

"Remember now," her voice was filled with a kind of rush of urgency, "no matter how hopeless you feel her situation is, don't give up. She must not die without God . . . without him. Promise you'll always pray?"

"I promise, Mother." It was an interesting lesson. There my mother lay dying of cancer and suffering terribly but wanting me to understand that Grace's dying without God would definitely be worse.

Furthermore, by asking me to pray for her sister, Mother gave me another project to help heal myself out of grief's self-centeredness and into positive actions relating to others. A little over ten years later my Aunt Grace and I had a marvelous conversation in a hospital ward, and not many months after that, she died at the age of fifty-seven like her sister Marion—but she left us to be with the Lord.

On the second day of the last week of Mother's life I caught on to another lesson. While my mother was no construction engineer, she wanted to leave me with a sturdy, well-built bridge to span the time between when she died and when we'd all meet again in heaven. Carefully she had gathered her materials. The bridge was to be made of one extremely important, yet simple, message. She constructed it by using three words over and over again. Building went on at all hours of the day and night.

"Joyce-Honey?"

"Yes, Mother."

"Are you still here?"

"Mmmm."

"What are you doing over there?"

"Nothing. I'm just here."

"Is it night or morning?"

"It's 2:30 in the morning, Mother."

"Honey?"

"Yes."

"I love you."

"I love you too, Mother."

Another time, as I was leaving to get a cup of coffee in the cafeteria, she called out and built another section of the bridge. "Honey?"

"Yes, Mother."

"Are you leaving or going away?"

"Well, I'm not going away or home, I'm just going to get a cup of coffee downstairs."

"Oh."

I had just stepped into the hall when I heard her add, "Joyce-Honey, you are loved." Mother was doing a beautiful yet strange thing. As nearly as I could tell, she was building a bridge simply with the words "I love you." She constructed it toward me; yet at the same time, she seemed to be slowly detaching herself from me. It was a bridge that could be traveled both ways. She was loving me and all our family while she was cutting the ties. I could feel that the spoken words "I love you" were followed by the silent, implied word *good-bye*. Each of us who stood by her bedside was to hear her words of love followed by her words of farewell.

Many other people have told me that in their conversations with the dying the words "I love you" are emphatically repeated over and over again. It's that two-way bridge again. I find it very moving that after all is said and done, the words *I love you* end up being the most important words in the whole world left to say.

When my friend Marilu's young son was injured in a bicycle accident, he underwent two brain surgeries to relieve hemorrhaging. In the hours that followed he was only conscious for a few seconds, but before he died he built the same bridge. He called, "Mama . . . Mama?" Marilu touched his arm and said, "I'm right here, honey." He responded with, "Oh, Mama, I love you." The dying know they're dying; and they want "I love you," their most important message, to be remembered.

On the third day of her last week my mother taught me about a Christian's sense of humor. Three decades later, this lesson still makes me smile and helps to heal my own days with a lovely joy. I had left Mother's room while she was dozing. The cafeteria was almost empty. I was too late for breakfast and too early for lunch, so I had two cups of coffee and, since I love doughnuts, I finished off their last, rather stale one.

When I came back to Mother's room her door was closed. It didn't register with me that the door might be closed for a reason. I pushed on through it and froze in my tracks at what I saw.

My mother was turned on her side, her back toward me, and two nurses were on the other side of the bed facing her and holding her hands. Two doctors at Mother's back were concentrating on inserting two ugly-looking drainage tubes. Large glass bottles on the floor were hooked up to those tubes. (The procedure they were starting is called thoracentesis, the treatment to pump and drain the build-up of fluid from the lungs and chest cavity.) While she had received this treatment several times during the past year, I'd never seen it and never been allowed into the room while it was being done. Hastily, I said, "Whoops, I'm sorry—" and started to back out the door.

"Don't go. I want you to sit right there and watch this," the senior doctor ordered. I sat. *Is he kidding?* I thought. *What does he hope to accomplish by my seeing this?* My mother's hands were being held by the two nurses, and I could see she was gripping them hard because of the pain. Her knuckles showed white through the taut skin. I could hardly bear to see her in such agony.

After the doctors had adjusted the tubes once more, Dr. Collins straightened up, looked directly at me, and announced sternly and abruptly, "Joyce, I never want to see you in this place as a patient with advanced breast cancer." His hand gently patted my mother's back. "She knew she had lumps for years, and she waited too long. This—" he waved his hands over the bottles, tubes, and drainage paraphernalia— "this is needless! I believe we could have saved her, but she waited too long." He was quite emotional and deeply agitated. I loved him deeply in those moments because he dropped the cold, professional mask of a medical authority and spoke as a human being concerned in loving care about my mother. This handsome Black doctor had been completely enchanted by my fifty-seven-year-old mother over the months he had known her and especially as he had treated her these past weeks.

He asked me if I had regular breast checkups. Mother said, "Doctor Honey, tell her again: I waited too long."

"I am, Mrs. Miller-Honey, I am," he answered.

When I wrote this chapter in 1974, I reported here that 32,000 women would die of breast cancer that year. Now, in 1994, the figure is 46,000 deaths each year from breast cancer. Many of these deaths including my mother's, as the doctor said, might have been prevented by early detection.

I sat there on a chair at the end of Mother's bed for another fifteen minutes, and then Dr. Collins motioned for me to take the nurses' place and hold Mother's hands. I'll never forget coming around the bed and being face to face with the visible evidence of her agony. There well may be a treat-ment procedure which is more painfully torturous, but I sin-cerely doubt it. Mother managed a small but wan smile up at me and whispered, "Is it almost over . . . are they almost through?" I looked across her shoulders at the doctors. Together they shook their heads and silently formed the word *no*. To Mother I lied and said, "It'll be just a little bit longer."

To make the time go faster, I asked her if I could do some-thing for her, read something or whatever. Mother quickly shook her head no, so I just stood by her bed and held her ashen-colored hands. I looked down into her face, and then to my utter surprise, her eyes were dancing as if they had heard a wild Hungarian rhapsody. She looked up at me and said excitedly, "Oh, I know! Joyce-Honey, you can sing for me!"

Without looking up I could see the doctors behind her. They had stopped their work and were staring at me. "What did you say, Mother?" I asked.

"I said sing for me."

I was caught off guard and was about to tell her I had prac-tically no voice at all when her doctor did it for me. "Oh, no, Mrs. Miller-Honey, Joyce has been here almost seven weeks around the clock. She's so tired she probably can't sing. Don't ask her to sing."

My mother's old, familiar, vivacious personality and vibrant sense of humor snapped, crackled, and popped through her brown eyes. She turned her head and shoulders backward just enough so she could see the doctors and said, "Listen here, Doctor-Honey, if you'd paid for as many voice lessons as I have . . . when I say sing, *she sings!*" The room fairly exploded with everyone's laughter.

"Atta girl, Mrs. Miller-Honey. Atta girl!" they laughed and said in unison to her.

To me they said, "*Sing!*"

It was amazing. Here was Mother, enduring several hours of unbelievable pain, and her well-developed sense of humor came through. It was a lesson I was never to forget.

Long before that scary day at her bedside she had taught me not to take myself too seriously. My mother did not want me to come unglued over the way life was shaping up for me or what it would be like in the future. What was happening to me was important, she had always said, but it wasn't the end of the world. That day my mother was dying and in prolonged agony, but she had God's confidence. She didn't want anyone to take all of this too seriously; after all, she *knew* where she was headed—to her heavenly home, with no more treatments like the one she was enduring.

I could hardly refuse her request, so I said, "Okay, what do you want me to sing?"

I was dreadfully weary, with very little voice left, and I didn't feel like singing anything. I felt like the captured people of Israel that the psalmist described when he wrote:

> Weeping, we sat beside the rivers of Babylon thinking of Jerusalem. We have put away our lyres, hanging them upon the branches of the willow tree, for how can we sing?
>
> Psalm 137:1–3

"How can we sing?" Good question, I thought. *How can I possibly pull myself together and sing?* But as I stood there looking at my mother's dear face and saw her bravery and courageous stamina, I thought, *I'd better* find *the voice to sing because if she can endure these tubes suctioning out the fluid in her chest with such good humor and love, the least I can do is sing my heart out for her!* Besides, there was the matter of all those voice lessons!

At this moment I wondered what I should sing. I would have guaranteed anyone that she would ask for either "His Eye Is on the Sparrow" or "My Heavenly Father Watches Over Me." So I mentally found the key and did a quick rehearsal of the words. When I asked her what song she wanted (even though I knew), she announced ever so instantly, "*The Sound of Music.*"

Stunned, I asked, "The song or the whole thing?"

Sweetly she answered, "The *whole* thing."

I certainly hadn't expected that, but I knew I had no business singing anything else, so I began this unexpected concert with "Do, Re, Mi" and moved on to "Sixteen Going On Seventeen." There in that hospital room, with doctors, nurses, tubes, equipment, and even a couple of cleaning women, I sang one song after another from that musical while she held tightly to my hands.

The windows had been opened, and a slight ocean breeze was drifting across the room. I saved "The Sound of Music" for my last song. As I went through the stanzas and into the final lyrics, Mother lifted and turned her head, ever so slightly, toward the windows, and the cool Pacific Ocean air seemed to gently fan her with a breath of fresh life. She bravely and yes, even majestically, sang the last four lines with me:

> I go to the hills when my heart is lonely,
> I know I will hear what I've heard before,
> My heart will be blessed with the sound of music
> And I'll sing once more.

As we sang, the realization swept over my soul that she didn't *need* the assurance or the comfort of such beautiful gospel songs as "His Eye Is on the Sparrow." She was already assured and comforted by God's love and had for many years known of God's love toward his children and his sparrows.

No wonder she asked me to sing *The Sound of Music;* she wanted to hear songs that would be a prologue to her homegoing. She knew she was soon to hear all the magnificent voices, choirs, and instruments of heaven. She wanted me to sing the prelude for the great heavenly concert that was about to begin for her.

Often in my musical lifetime we had discussed the incredible perfectness of heaven's music: the thousands of voices in the choirs, the equally large number of musicians in the orchestra, and how everyone would have absolutely stunning musical talent. No flat tenor voices, no wobbling tremolo soprano voices, no thin-toned altos, and no feeble bass voices. All would be perfect, just perfect. Except, of course, my mother would probably change keys in the middle of any song she sang—even in heaven—as she did here on earth.

In that hospital room, with her time here on earth obviously drawing to a close, Mother wanted to hear these last sounds knowing the next time we'd be together it would be in heaven, listening to heaven's sound of music. The closing song of that musical, *The Sound of Music*, became in those moments a hymn—one that's brought untold comfort to me and to many others who've heard me tell this story.

Later on that day, after the doctors had removed the tubes and taken away the bottles filled with fluid, Mother was not better as everyone had hoped. In fact, she seemed to have lost a lot of strength and was losing ground.

Patiently she adjusted to her new weakness. Once when she wakened I thought she said, "Joyce-Honey, push here . . . push here." I couldn't figure out what she meant by "push," and because she was so weak, she could barely communicate above a whisper. When she realized I didn't understand, she pulled herself together with great effort, and patting her chest, said, "Push . . . head here . . . we'll wait together." Finally I understood that she was trying to say *pray*, but it had come out *push*. I put my head on her chest and silently prayed. We waited together.

She slept, but I was too frightened to sleep. Mother was breathing in the extraordinary way the dying do, with long pauses between breaths. I'd never heard that kind of breathing, and it terrified me. One moment I would hear her steady, normal breathing, and then it would just stop. I would hear nothing. The seconds would mount up in what felt like years, and then, just as abruptly, she would simply resume her nor-

mal breathing. Once I panicked and ran to find the nearest
doctor, but when I asked him what was happening to Mother,
he muttered something about it not being too unusual. He
left me standing in the hall, knee-deep in unanswered, fearful questions.

Later on that morning I phoned a friend of mine and told
her how scary it was to listen to Mother's breathing because
I was never sure if it was her last breath. Bettye will never
know the measure of my relief when I heard her say, "Oh,
yes, I know about that breathing process. She must be breathing the Cheyenne-Stokes way. My father did that, too."

"What's *Cheyenne-Stokes?*" I asked.

In the next few minutes Bettye told me about the two doctors, Cheyenne and Stokes, who had discovered this kind of
breathing problem in the dying and done research on it. They
found that often the patient's respiratory center is so badly
affected that it causes highly irregular breathing. I wondered
why the doctor, when I asked him about Mother's unusual
breathing, hadn't told me that for the dying it was normal.
I suppose it's hard for doctors and nurses to understand that
lay people are nowhere near as knowledgeable in medicine
as they, or that what may be a common occurrence to a doctor may be a terribly frightening experience for people who
are seeing death for the first time and trying to cope with the
dying process of a loved one.

I will always be grateful to Pinkey, another friend of mine,
who was a nurse. She would patiently answer my frantic phone
calls when Mother's condition changed. If I didn't understand what was happening, I'd call Pinkey, and she'd give me
the explanations I needed. It was always easier to cope with
Mother's dying when I knew what it was I was trying to cope
with. It was the same way with my friend Bettye's explanation of the Cheyenne-Stokes breathing; once I understood
it, it was relatively easy to accept the phenomenon later when
it occurred over and over again. I didn't panic quite so quickly
or so often.

The fourth day came and went uneventfully, but on the fifth day of that week my mother quietly but determinedly announced, "I want to go home." She made her request to me and everyone who came near her. By the time she asked her favorite "Doctor-Honey," to my surprise, Doctor-Honey said, "Your mother wants to go home." I was grateful to him because he had listened to her and believed her.

"Do you take full responsibility for her?" he asked me. When I nodded yes, he wrote out a release form that stated Mother could go home for twenty-four to forty-eight hours, depending on how long she wanted to stay. He told me that I'd have to bring her back after that.

My father, brother, and sister all scurried around, readied up the house, rented an oxygen tank—the "Bird"—and other equipment, and finally, borrowed the Walstroms' (dear people in my dad's congregation) new station wagon. Gently Mother was placed on foam-rubber pads, and we took her home that afternoon.

My brother and Dad brought her into the house amid much laughing and fun scolding. It was a welcome release of tension to laugh, and she helped us all by winking at me and saying, "I know they're gonna drop me!" They managed not to fulfill her prediction and placed her in the living room on an outdoor chaise lounge with wheels.

I think it was exactly at that moment it dawned on me why it was so terribly important to her to come home. I believe it was a part of unfinished business that she felt she had to take care of. It was her time to say a meaningful and proper good-bye to all of us. Nowadays, psychologists call it closure.

Almost seven weeks earlier, Mother had left her home, left us, left her furniture and things, even left her favorite little dog, Buttons. She and everyone else had fully expected her to be home in a few days. Now she understood she'd be leaving forever, and dearest to her heart was the desire to say her loving farewells to all of us and for one last time to be surrounded by the familiarity of her earthly home.

"Mother," I said as it occurred to me, "you want to go into all the rooms, don't you?"

"Oh, yes," she responded. "Take me." So Marilyn and I pushed her down the hall past bedrooms and bathroom, stopping long enough for her to glimpse inside each room and whisper her faint good-byes. We turned her around, pushed her back down the hall, let her stay in the center of her kitchen for a few minutes, and then rolled her narrow bed into the dining room. For a moment she looked at her dish cabinet and then, longingly, she looked outside through the sliding glass doors toward the swimming pool we had all had so much fun in and around.

"You want to go out there, too, don't you?" I asked. Instantly she nodded yes. The September sun in California was broiling the backyard plants to dry crispiness, but she lay out there for a few minutes letting its penetrating heat warm up her death-chilled bones. When she had seen enough, we took her back inside, through the dining room to the living room. As we got to the piano, Mother asked us to stop, and looking at my sister, said, "Marilyn-Honey, I want you to play one more song for me."

The circle of farewells was now completed. She had said good-bye to all of us, to the rooms, and even to the swimming pool. With the exception of my brother (who is not too terribly musical), all of us had sung for her. My singing of *The Sound of Music*, my father's songs to her weeks before, and now my sister's note-perfect classical piano playing had completed the sound of music on this earth. She asked to be taken to the den so she could rest.

As darkness came to the San Fernando Valley, I fixed up some blankets on the floor beside Mother's bed. My brother and I worked out a schedule where one of us would be awake with her throughout the night. We alternated every two hours. Around five or six in the morning I sent Cliff off to bed and took my third or fourth shift. Neither of us turned on any lights; we came and went all during the night, awake and listening to her faulty breathing.

My mother seemed to be sleeping lightly, so I lay back on my blankets and waited for daybreak, wondering what new sadness the day would bring and how long the dying process could continue. Suddenly out of the darkness Mother's hand came tapping down my arm, back up again toward my neck and face, and I heard her ask, "Who's down there? . . . Who do I have now?"

"It's me—Joyce," I answered. Her humor flickered for a moment as she chuckled a bit and said, "I wasn't sure, you know; there's been a lot of coming and going around here lately!"

We both lay there with the faint light of the new dawn breaking through the window, and then in the stillness I heard her voice. Calmly and with no apparent breathing difficulties, she said quietly, "Joyce-Honey, I'm going home . . . soon."

"Yes, Mother." I was nowhere near as calm as she, but I came up with, "Just think, you'll see Jesus soon."

"Not soon enough," she responded. "I want to go home *now*, honey."

"I know, Mother . . . I know."

She gradually drifted off to sleep. Later, when the room was lighter, I saw her hand as it came down off the bed and groped for my shoulder. She tapped me and said, "If that's still you, Joyce-Honey, *pray!*"

Not only did I experience the dawning of the sun that morning, the sixth day of her last week, but also the dawning of a horrible realization: I remembered I had a speaking engagement that noon. I had not canceled it earlier because the event was so far into September that I had been sure by then I'd be back on my regular schedule. I'd completely forgotten the event. I don't know why I remembered it, other than the Lord had jogged my memory. Somehow I felt it was important to go, but I couldn't bear thinking of leaving Mother.

I sat up, and touching her face, told her that I was scheduled to speak for her local Christian Businesswoman's Club luncheon. I asked if she minded if I left her and went. I should have known her response. She urgently assured me that I *had* to go. Amazingly, her mind was clear enough to tell me to say hello to Frances Eliers, who would be there.

Reluctantly, I got up and left her to get dressed. When I was all ready to leave I went in to see if she was all right, and she said she needed a bedpan. So I took care of her needs and was leaving the room, all dressed up for the luncheon and carrying out her used bedpan, when she looked up, smiled, and remarked, "Ah, yes, you should write a book called *From Bedpan to Banquet* by Joyce Landorf." Her humor helped me go. I don't remember what I spoke on or even if I sang (I doubt it), but since the luncheon was for a local chapter and my mother had attended it regularly, I recall that many of her personal friends came to the head table to speak of their love for Marion and to assure me of their prayers. Those precious women did not preach or fumble for words; they simply said, "I love her, too." Their words formed an instant support group around my heart and gave me the most marvelous uplift for my dragging spirits.

I drove back to my parents' house after the luncheon, and my Aunt Grace and grandmother were there. It was a scene I froze in my memory so I'd never forget. My grandmother was sitting on the edge of the bed holding my mother's hand, and Aunt Grace was leaning against the wall. They spoke in Hungarian, and what I didn't understand my aunt later filled in for me.

My grandmother said, "Mutishka [Marion], my daughter, are you dying?"

Mother instantly nodded her head yes.

"Mutishka, are you afraid of death?"

Mother gave a slight smile and said, "No, Mama."

Grandma stood up and said, "Good. Now I give her to God. I go now." Then she picked up her little black hat, jammed it down on the top of her head, pinned it with a hatpin like all little old ladies did, and said to Grace, "Come, we go now. We wait at home." Looking at me she said in broken English, "You call me when she go."

Ah, there it was again: confidence. Long after Grandma and Aunt Grace left that day, my mother's mouth showed the traces of a smile because of that dear conversation. Hand in hand, confidence and closure took place.

Marilyn and my daughter, Laurie, were at the house that day, and I asked them to try not to cry when they were with Mother. It was a mistake on my part, but (in my defense) I know now that I was fiercely protective of Mother, and I felt it would be terribly upsetting to Mother if both girls gave way to tears. My lecture didn't work too well, however. Laurie (then eleven) took one look at her beloved grandmother, and her whole face gave away her emotions. She burst into tears and fled into Marilyn's bedroom to sob her heart out.

Mother was puzzled and asked, "What in the world is the matter with Laurie? I couldn't get a word out of her." I explained that Laurie's love for her was very deep and that when Laurie saw her she realized that her grandmother was going to heaven soon. It was too much for my sensitive-to-others Laurie. Mother nodded her head and smiled a knowing smile. Then my sister came in, and Mother took the matter of her death into her own hands. She pulled my little sister close to her and said, "Marilyn-Honey, this disease will not heal. I'm not going to get well." My sister, unable to hold the flow of tears back (again in spite of my instructions), put her head down on Mother's stomach and sobbed out the burning question, "Mother, Mother, why is God doing this?" Very firmly but quietly Mother answered, "I don't know, honey, I don't know." The two stayed there without moving or talking, and the stillness of that hour was broken only by my sister's muffled sobbing.

We may all find ourselves in the place of not knowing or understanding the whys of death, but it is important to realize that when one like Mother is dying and says "I don't know," she says it without fear, without bitterness, and without frustration or anger. Her words, spoken so long ago, have tenderly touched my heart over the years. There is much in this world that we don't know or can't explain. It's not a question of having all the answers at our fingertips but giving those unanswerable details over to the Lord. We need to entrust to God our painful whys and then watch his quiet peace erase the fear, bitterness, frustration, and anger from the blackboards of our minds.

When my mother asked God her whys, he did not answer them but gave to her instead a genuine measure of peaceful confidence to tide her over. It was enough for her then and it remains enough for all of us now.

That day Mother showed us that a Christian dies not only in quiet confidence, but with forgiveness up to date. It happened after I'd returned home from my speaking engagement. She had been dozing later that afternoon, when she suddenly woke up, and seeing me by her bedside, startled me with, "Joyce, have I been a good mother to you?"

The question was so easy to answer that I laughed out loud at her asking it. "Oh, Mother," I said with a chuckle, "you have been the kind of biblical mother whose children 'rise up and call her *blessed!*' All of us—Cliff, Marilyn, even your grandchildren—we all rise up and call you blessed, and for the rest of our lives we will always remember how wonderful you were as a mother and grandmother."

But she was not amused or smiling; in fact, she was shaking her head slowly and forming the words, "No . . . that's not true."

"Joyce-Honey," she stated flatly, "I've failed you."

"No. No," I protested. "Mother, if you have, I can't remember it and even if you *did* fail, it doesn't matter now!" I thought I was successful in shushing her up, but she wouldn't be shushed.

"I failed you at least once, I remember," she said sadly. "I failed you when David died. Remember? I didn't come to the funeral." Without letting me say anything, she plunged

right on. "I made a terrible mistake then, Joyce; I should
have been there." Her eyes filled with tears, and she turned
to look directly into my eyes and asked, "Honey, will you
ever forgive me for not going to little David's funeral?"

"Oh, Mother," by now I was sobbing, "I already have forgiven you. I did it a short time after David died. I admit that
I was hurt by Daddy and you not coming, but I stopped trying in my own strength to forgive you, and I was finally able
to let God work a forgiveness through me. The forgiving has
all been done, and it's all right." The beauty of the moment
was incredible. (Now that I have grown children of my own,
I know it takes mature parents to admit to their child that
they were wrong; but it takes a humble and mature parent
to follow this admission with the words, "Will you forgive
me?") My mother wanted to die with the assurance that old
hurts were healed and that she'd asked forgiveness, as she felt
was fitting for a Christian.

It was near evening when her breathing, even with the help
of the machines, started going badly. She was obviously
becoming more and more distressed and unable to get suf-
ficient air into her lungs. Her words rasped out to me: "Joyce-
Honey, tell me, how are you praying for me?"

There was no way I could possibly tell her exactly how I
was praying. I felt it would sound too cold and far too unlov-
ing. Mother's physical agony was lasting beyond anyone's
concept of endurance, so many of Mother's friends and I
were praying that God would end her suffering. "Pray that
it will be today," we sadly agreed. To those of you who have
never waited on the dying process, I'm sure that on the surface that kind of praying sounds rather insensitive. I don't
believe it is, however, especially in view of prolonged pain.
Praying for the dying one's release becomes the only prayer
to pray. But when Mother asked me that afternoon to tell
her truthfully how I was praying for her, I was unable to
speak. When I hesitated too long, she asked again, "Tell me,
how are you praying?"

Deliberately evading the truth, I said, "Well, I'm praying that the Lord's will be done." I'll never forget her instant response.

A look of complete disgust passed across her face, and with a great deal of scorn in her voice she rebuked me with, "Well, you stop that prayer this instant! That's the wrong way to pray!"

"It is?" I meekly backed down.

"It certainly is. You ask the Lord to take me home. This—" she began coughing—"this has gone on too long." She took several deep breaths from the oxygen mask and then finished with me by saying, "Tell him to hurry up. I'm past due!"

I don't know if she sensed I'd been less than honest about the content of my prayers, but I'm sure she wanted me to know that she was ready to die and wasn't about to be wrapped up and protected by well-meaning lies or half-truths. She wanted to die in total honesty. She knew it was time to leave us. She also wanted me to stop hindering her home-going. After Mother had taught me her lesson on how to pray for the dying, she quietly dismissed me by falling asleep.

An hour or so later she stirred, and I asked her if she wanted me to get her anything or to read to her. She understood me and said, "Yes, something from Philippians." I opened to Philippians and asked, "Any particular place, Mother?" She lifted her hand in a gesture that said it didn't matter. I looked down and was startled by the first line I saw. It was as if she'd planned for me to open to that passage. I read aloud:

> But whatever happens to me, remember always to live as Christians should, so that, whether I ever see you again or not, I will keep on hearing good reports that you are standing side by side with one strong purpose— to tell the Good News fearlessly, no matter what your enemies may do.
>
> Philippians 1:27

Mother put her hand over the pages, so I stopped reading and looked over at her. She was smiling, and barely wagging a finger at me, she admonished, "I'll be listening for all those good reports!" Then she motioned for me to continue reading. About the time I was reading verse thirty in the same chapter ("We are in this fight together. You have seen me suffer for him in the past; and I am still in the midst of a great and terrible struggle now, as you know so well"), Mother said softly, "No more."

I took notes that afternoon, and the last line on my scribbled page was written after I'd read Philippians. I wrote

But, yes, dear Mother, I've seen you suffering, but always you have been utterly fearless! Thank God for his confidence.

Not too long after that I met with Cliff in the long hall outside her door. We discussed her breathing, and since both of us felt it was much worse we decided it was time for her to return to the hospital. I went into her room, touched her face, and asked her if she wanted to go back to the hospital. Immediately she opened her eyes and answered, "Yes. *Now.*"

My dad, brother, sister, and I were just getting her settled on the foam-rubber pads in the back of the station wagon when my Aunt Ellen (my father's sister), Uncle Greg, and some of our cousins from Michigan pulled up in the driveway behind us. It was mass confusion because none of us had seen each other for years, and unfortunately, Dad's letters had never told them the seriousness of Mother's illness. They had no idea Mother was sick, much less dying.

In all the noisy confusion with my aunt, uncle, cousins, and a brand-new baby, I bent over Mother and told her I would stay there at home with everybody. I assured her that I'd see her in the morning. The next memory is still very painful. As her mind registered what I was saying, she shook her head in a definite no. It was a strong, stubborn, authority-filled *no,* and I couldn't understand why she said it with such angry vehemence.

I bent over and kissed her quickly and said, "Mother, it's all right. I'll see you in the morning. Aunt Ellen and Uncle Greg have come all this way, and someone better stay with them. Okay?" She closed her eyes and didn't answer me. I wish I'd known what she knew at that moment: that sometimes the dying have no more I'll-see-you-in-the-mornings left.

My dad, brother, and sister drove Mother out of the driveway, and I went into the house to explain to my shocked and saddened relatives that I felt Mother had precious little time left. I was still talking to everybody in the living room when Dad, Cliff, and Marilyn returned from the hospital. Dad reported Mother was all settled and had bid them all good night. She had even sent them cheerfully on their way. I was just asking Dad about how she handled the trip back to the hospital when the phone rang.

The call was for me. My husband had decided he didn't want me to stay at my parents' house overnight or go on over to the hospital that night as I'd planned. He told me I had to come home. "Our children need you, and I need you," he argued. I was desperate for rest, but I felt the end for Mother was imminent. He countered by reminding me that I'd been there almost seven weeks, coming home only occasionally, and that she was still living. We had a quick but forceful argument, and in the end I gave in and agreed to go home.

On the Santa Monica freeway, the exit I usually took to UCLA Medical Center loomed ahead. It was nearly midnight and there was almost no traffic. I hesitated and could have turned off, but at the last second, for reasons I can never understand, I continued straight ahead and drove home. I asked God to keep Mother here until I could go back the next day, and I sank into my own bed, completely exhausted.

The first ring of the phone next to our bed startled us, and we awoke instantly. It was light in our room and not quite

7:00 A.M. My husband answered before the second ring. Without saying too much, he listened and then replaced the phone on its stand.

"That was Dad. The hospital said she died in her sleep this morning at 6:34."

"Thank God," breathed out of the haziness of sleep from somewhere inside of me. But then as I opened my eyes fully, I was aware of the sunlight flooding the bedroom. Anguished thoughts began to form and then to scream inside me. *Oh, Mother, it's morning, and after all that waiting and watching, I didn't get to see you go! I wasn't there . . . and now it's morning. You went without me! I wanted to be there. Oh, dear God, no!* My mother had known the night before that she'd run out of mornings. She had tried to tell me. But I hadn't listened and had left her. I didn't see her go. I had *meant* to be there. Over and over the knife of regret struck at me, and when there was nothing left to strike at, it stayed on stirring the slush of what was left of my heart.

Grandfather

He looked through me,
His eyes heavy with death.

He did not say, but wished to say:
"Open the window."

So I opened the window
And turned to tell him
It was useless to try and drag himself
The impossible distance to where he might
Also look across the fields and fences
Toward the woods
Of his Sunday afternoon wanderings.

I turned to tell him
The birds were building new nests

Upon the sites of the old,
And that the little river had shifted again,
But Grandfather left me by the window
And went himself
To see about the things I meant to tell him.

                                               Robert M. Howell

Not being with my mother when she died has had a profound effect on my life. I still feel the sting of my regrets.
Only recently, in dealing with cancer and trying to find ways
to help heal my body and my mind, did I realize that what
hurt me the most in not being with my mother when she
died is that I never was able to bring closure to her death. I
also never was able to bring closure to David's death, as I
didn't get to hold him or see him after he died.

Not too many years ago at my father's graveside, I knelt
by my mother's headstone and finally was able to bring closure to that emotionally expensive experience. Just this past
month, while I was out to California visiting my children,
my husband Francis and I, along with my granddaughter Jen-
nifer, went out to the cemetary in Pomona where David had
been cremated. Just being there brought a measure of closure to my heart, closure which eases my memories and my
loneliness until I see them again.

8

Majestic Mourning Song

Hush li'l baby, don't you cry
You know your mama was born to die
All my trials Lord, soon be over.
All my trials Lord, soon be over.

Jordan river is chilly and cold,
Chills the body but not the soul,
All my trials Lord, soon be over.
All my trials Lord, soon be over.

Traditional Spiritual

For those of us left behind to pick up the jagged pieces of our broken lives, can there be any songs to sing? Will there ever be a time when we stop feeling the ripping apart that continues inside our hearts? A friend said of her pain after her twenty-six-year-old son was killed in an auto accident, "I felt like I had a toothache raging all through my entire body." Can we ever begin to respond to others and function in our daily routines in what we once knew as a normal way? Since the experience of losing a loved one is so devastating, the

immediate answers to these questions seem to be no—
unequivocally *no.*

Yet at the same instant we call out *no,* coming from deep
within us spontaneously, almost involuntarily, rises a motion
of hope. And almost as if it were from a distance, we hear
ourselves say, *Wait a minute, aren't you God's child?* If the
response to that question is yes, then perhaps we need to
hang on and to grab hold of God's words. He said, "I'll not
leave you comfortless." Didn't he promise to help us walk
this dark valley? Of course he did, and he has given his Word
for our safe passage to life and its normality.

I believe that what God really promised is to give us a song,
a song he plays for us even in the midst of death and sorrow.
It probably won't be the frivolous, New Orleans jazz-band
music that's often played at funerals and wakes; more likely
it will be a quiet song full of confidence, a song fitting enough
for a bridal procession, exciting enough for a New Year's Day
parade, and majestic enough for a king's coronation day. It
will be an orchestrated song for full symphony, with its incredible beauty; a song which will not disappear into the night
but will be heard by us forever.

When it comes, we almost do not dare listen to it. It sounds
too good to be true, and we think, *Music out of all of this?*
We are alone, and we feel forever abandoned. We have lost
someone, and in the losing we have been sliced in half. We
cannot imagine being a whole person again; it is almost too
much to believe in or hope for. People around us tell us, "Get
on with your life," but right now it's hard to know what that
means since grief is such a dark, mysterious emotion.

But *God* is not dead; and when we, his children, experience the death of a loved one and feel the sorrow that fol-
lows, or fear our own imminent death, God begins his majestic mourning song in the quiet places of our hearts and minds.
To hear it is to breathe again. At first the song seems strange
and remote, but gradually we realize we *can* hear it, for it *is*
here.

The morning my mother died I think I heard the song faintly, but it was drowned out by two pressing obligations. The first was a writing assignment: I was writing for Biola University's magazine, and my column was past due. Other than that I felt I should write about my mother's homegoing, I had no other creative ideas.

The second was funeral arrangements. My father was still in denial and had phoned to tell me he'd be waiting at his home for me to come over; I was designated as the one to make all the necessary arrangements. I had little or no desire to do this and thought about how terribly drained I felt. Everything within me was fatigued beyond belief.

Just as I was getting dressed to go to Dad's house, I grabbed (almost absentmindedly) a piece of paper and a pen that were on my nightstand. Before I knew it, these words flowed out on to the paper. To the background of grief's quiet music in my soul, in the midst of trying to get ready to leave, the text for my magazine column appeared:

> Right now the angels of heaven are rushing through those golden corridors, shouting, "Marion is here, Marion is here!"
>
> In my mind's eye, I can see all of heaven assembling in the great hall. Angels, saints of the Old Testament, our Lord, and of course, the new one, Marion.
>
> Marion, born in 1909 of such humble beginnings in a little village east of Budapest, Hungary, and brought to this country as a little girl, now stands in heaven!
>
> I imagine she is impatient a little as she wants to join the choir. And join she will! It may take a few days for the director to figure it out, but soon he will complain to his superior music-master that "Marion sings off key."
>
> The complaint will reach the higher-ups, and then the word will come back, "She must stay in the choir and

yes, in the front row, even though she can't carry a tune."

"Why?" comes the gentle question of the director.

"Well, it seems for most of her fifty-seven years on earth she has sung her praises to the Lord," is the reply.

She has introduced hundreds of children to the Master by her loving work in Sunday school, daily vacation Bible school, Child Evangelism classes and many summer weeks at "Good News" camps.

She has worked physically, mentally, and spiritually side by side with her minister husband for almost thirty-eight years, sharing all the joys and all the heartaches of the ministry.

She has been a mother whose three children "rise up and call her blessed."

By her exciting Bible classes and her chaplaincy in the Christian sorority, Lambda Theta Chi, she has helped countless women to trust in Christ. By her everyday living she has inspired even more men and women to give God only their very best.

Always she has sung her song of praise. (Yes, "off key." Sometimes she has changed keys nine times in one chorus of "In My Heart There Rings a Melody.") The Lord, however, says it is the sweetest sound he heard coming from earth so she is to continue her song in the choir as before. Heaven wouldn't be right without that sweet "off-key" voice.

The great hall is filled now, all of heaven has gathered, and the angels have finished their magnificent songs of praise; and all are standing quietly, with folded wings, for they are listening to Marion.

What are the words to that beautiful song?

> Holy, Holy is what the angels sing,
> And I expect to help them make
>   the courts of heaven ring.
> But when I tell redemption's story
> They will fold their wings.
> For angels never felt the joys
> That our salvation brings.

So with her gentle humor and her exciting way of talking she is telling them how she went from "sinner" to "saved" and all about the "joys salvation brought."

Heaven glistens a little brighter today because Marion Miller, my mother, is there.

The Lord, in the moments it took to write those words, began his first move toward healing me. I had begun to hear his music. He helped me laugh a bit as I reread my article, especially when he reminded me of my mother's inability to stay on key. All the times I'd tried to imitate her but couldn't were flashed back through my mind, and it was a warm, happy memory. The warmth of those moments was short-lived. Within the hour my husband and I left our home and made our way across Los Angeles to begin making funeral arrangements.

My dad met us at his front door, and together we took our last journey over to UCLA Medical Center. It was strange going there this time, and when I reached the third floor I automatically went straight down the hall into my mother's room. I was stunned and stopped short by the empty, immaculate, and very sterile-looking room. The bed was newly made up and Mother was gone. The absence of not only Mother, but also all the equipment, was mind boggling. The room was devoid of any human personality. It was a barren place, impersonal and cold. I must have experienced some of the same feelings the disciples of Jesus felt when they looked into his tomb and found it empty. "He is not here, He is risen" (see Matt. 28:6 KJV), they were told. I know how blank and numb their minds must have gone at that instant.

I leaned against the doorjamb and tried to figure it out. I finally thought, *She isn't here. I wonder why I looked for her? Mother's gone. She is with God.* I turned out of the doorway into the hall and bumped into Mother's favorite Doctor-Honey. All I could say was, "She's gone." My words were filled with a bewildered kind of acceptance.

Dr. Collins leaned up against the wall and responded, "I didn't know. I wasn't in the ward this morning. I didn't know until now." The tears were streaming down his face as he talked, and he made no effort to dry them. He said, "I've only known her for the past few months. I wish to God I'd known her my whole lifetime like you have." When he realized that I'd seen his tears, he apologized and said that crying was highly unprofessional of him, but that he had loved Mrs. Miller-Honey. I mumbled something about us all loving her, since she was easy to love.

We stepped over to the desk, and I filled in some things on several hospital forms. I signed the autopsy permission papers and re-lived the moment I had with David's autopsy forms. But I didn't hesitate to sign; my mother had spent her life giving to others, and I wanted to let her go on serving others even in death. I donated her eyes to UCLA's famous eye bank. The last thing I wrote on one of those papers was her age. When the doctor looked at it he said, "Joyce, your mother wasn't thirty-four."

"Whoops." I hastily corrected it to fifty-seven and said, "I don't know why I wrote down my own age instead of hers, other than I've always thought of us as being exactly the same age." My mother had been a "becomer," as Keith Miller would have called her had he known her. She was not an "arriver," or one who knew everything about anything with no more need to learn. She was young at heart, and life was full of new adventures and new lessons for her to learn. Most often her phone conversations with me started out with, "Well, Joyce-Honey, what new and wonderful thing has God done for you today?" To think of her as not only fifty-seven years old, but *gone* as well, was very difficult. Denial in those moments was easy.

Her body was somewhere in the morgue at the hospital, but of course I didn't see her that day. I walked down the corridor listening to the sweet, sad symphony of my mourning song that was beginning to crescendo in my heart. The reason to come to that place on the third floor had disappeared. And strange as it seemed, that day I was bittersweet-sad to leave it. The hospital had become my home. Its doctors, nurses, and other staff members had been kind to my mother. Many of them had fallen in love with Mrs. Miller-Honey. In my memory's ear I still hear the doctors in the corridors of that hospital as they called out to each other, "Did you hear what Mrs. Miller-Honey said today?" Even in dying she had reached out in God's love and transformed the lives of those around her. She would not soon be forgotten. I was reluctant to leave, when all was said and done; it was as if I were leaving home for good. It would be strange to never return there . . . but I never did.

After leaving the hospital, I went back to Dad's home to plan the funeral. It is no wonder that funeral arrangements are so baffling to most of us. We are asked to make so many decisions just when we have experienced the most frightening loss in our lives. Our minds are fragmented like shattered glass on a tile floor.

Suddenly we find, as much as we'd like to stay hidden within the confines of shock and denial, we must rouse ourselves and come forward to pick out a casket, select a dress or a suit, drive it over to the mortuary, and decide what type of service is most appropriate. These are just a few of the surface things that must be done.

When my son David died, I was still in the hospital recovering from the cesarean-section surgery, so my husband made all of David's funeral arrangements. We were fortunate that our local mortician was tremendously helpful. He knew me from when I had sung at many funerals at that mortuary and our large church, so he knew of our huge medical expenses that had piled up that year. He listed each price range (for casket, burial, etc.) and suggested ways to cut funeral costs way down. I am still indebted to Todd's Mortuary for all the gentle kindness its director and staff extended to us.

My experience with a mortuary in a different city, when my grandfather died a year later, was exactly the opposite. I accompanied my Aunt Grace to the mortuary to make arrangements and pick out a casket for Grandpa. The large, cold room (I don't know why it wasn't heated) filled with caskets was more frightening than a monster movie. Our nerves and emotions were ravaged as it was, but to stand amid twenty or thirty empty caskets was hard to accept. I could not take my eyes off a small blue-and-white baby's casket. It would have fit David so well. The pain of the moment penetrated my soul without mercy.

That pain was nothing, however, compared to the pain the mortician inflicted on us. First of all, he was as jovial as a master of ceremonies for a festive banquet and about twice as phony. It was quite irritating to both Aunt Grace and me. He came up behind my aunt and said in his pseudo-friendly voice, "Well, now, how are we coming along?" Without waiting for a reply he glanced at the casket my aunt was studying and said, "Oh, no, my dear, you don't want to put Papa in that *cheap* casket. Put him in this one over here."

My first thought was that he had absolutely no right to call my grandpa "Papa." It should be "Mr. Uzon" to him, but my second thought blurted out of me before I could stop it.

"How much *is* that 'cheap casket' we *don't* want for Papa?" I asked. He muttered something about it being nine hundred dollars and said again that he didn't think it would do for Papa.

I remember firmly taking Aunt Grace's arm, and knowing Grandpa only had about one thousand dollars from insurance to bury himself, I whispered to her, "I think *that one* will do very well for our beautiful Papa. Because in the first place, he's not really *here*, but with the Lord; and in the second place, he didn't have a ton of money."

My aunt was sick with grief and had no heart for discussing or haggling over prices, and no one took more advantage of the situation than the mortician. I still feel angry when I remember how the man made Aunt Grace feel guilty about one casket and feel obligated to buy another more expensive one.

At the time of death there are many factors that arise, and cost is certainly one of them, yet we must try not to lose sight of the message of life and hope we have as Christians. We must not fail to take into consideration the deceased person's life, attitudes, and yes, economic position. A father's death may have been preceded by years of financial strain due to medical bills. Or this may have been a woman's fourth miscarriage of a late-term baby. To have someone irresponsibly increase those financial burdens is morally wrong.

Much has been said about funerals, mortuaries, and mourners over the years, but I think some of the best things said about Christians and funerals are said by Joe Bayly in *The View From a Hearse* and by Gladys Hunt in her book *The Christian Way of Death*. Gladys Hunt sums up my feelings on funerals when she states, "In the final analysis, a Christian funeral is not determined by cost or efficiency, but by the message it proclaims."

If the death is a sudden one, if there was no will, if all funds were in one name and not in a joint checking account, or if all insurance papers were kept secret, all the bereaved can see is the horrendous amount of red tape they'll have to work through; and all of this comes on top of their grief. One widow stated starkly, "I never knew there was so much paper work, red tape, and decisions to be made in the *whole* world!"

Stephanie, the young widow who talked with me about her husband's death, said, "The only thing that helped me with all those funeral arrangements was that John and I had discussed what we would want when either of us died." When I asked her what she would say to other young couples about the lessons of grief, she said, "Oh, early in their marriage the couple should discuss their future, including the possibility of their own deaths. They should be well read-up on death and dying." Then she shared how much her chance reading about autopsy in the *Reader's Digest* had prepared her to immediately say yes about her husband's autopsy. "It was much easier to sign those papers after knowing about the importance of autopsies," she said.

Stephanie clearly heard her own song of mourning, and in the beautiful memorial bulletin for her husband's service she wrote these lines:

My Song

Praise to the Lord for
the difference He made
in John's life.

Praise to the Lord for
sparing him in length
of illness.

Praise to the Lord for
the family He chose John
to come from.

Praise to the Lord for
the friends we have.

Praise, praise to the Lord
for leading John to
marry me.

Praise to the Lord for
letting us choose our
eternal future.

"Even so, come, Lord Jesus."
Revelation 22:20 (KJV)

It was not the color or cost of John's casket, or the amount of money given to his memorial fund, but the proclamation of the radiant Christian message given at the service that turned his service into something very beautiful and touching.

My mother had never discussed her funeral with me, but we had talked so many times of other services that I felt I knew what she wanted. She'd attended hundreds of funerals, and I knew she wanted a message of hope for those left behind. She also wanted her service to be held in Dad's church, *not* at a mortuary. She wanted it to be at the church because that was the place where she'd served and worked. I also knew of her great love of flowers and knew that she would want to be surrounded with their beauty. So, with the help of many other people the service was arranged in these ways.

In my book *The Richest Lady in Town* I described her memorial service:

> Breast cancer took everything from her except the sparkling spirit that fairly danced out of her dark brown eyes. In less than three years after her mastectomy and halfway through her fifty-seventh year, the Lord said, "That is absolutely all the pain I will allow her to bear," and He issued the command for Death to bring her to Him.
>
> She went more than willingly, but we let her go with halting reluctance. We dressed her in her favorite flowered voile dress, surrounded her with a huge garden of flowers and packed in Dad's church with hundreds of people who listened to her funeral service.

John Gustafson's voice rang out in her favorite songs,
"Until Then" and "My Heavenly Father Watches Over
Me"; Chuck Leviton read a poem he had composed
about her, "Marion Miller, The Quiet Fanatic."

Here's Chuck Leviton's poem:

> I'd call her a quiet fanatic,
> One whose life had been changed,
> Who had come face to face with the Master
> And since had not been the same.
>
> Yes, she was a quiet fanatic,
> With consistency serving the King,
> She lived for a brighter tomorrow,
> With heart full of faith she sang.
>
> She lived for a brighter tomorrow
> While serving the King today,
> Her heart was in touch with the Master
> And changes occurred when she prayed.
>
> She was not a wide-eyed fanatic
> Ranting and raving a creed,
> But one of quiet dedication,
> Reminding a world of its need.
>
> She was a person of selfless denial,
> Living a labor of love,
> I'm talking of Marion Miller,
> Whose heart had been touched from above.
>
> She was a Christian of real compassion,
> Whose power in prayer was alive,
> Who tenderly loved the unlovely
> Whose passion cannot be denied.
>
> Thank God for Marion Miller,
> Whose life was a blessing to all,

While life here has ceased for Marion,
Her blessings live on and on.

God used this quiet fanatic,
This vessel through which He flowed,
Lord, thank you for Marion Miller,
She was a privilege to know.

Dr. Ted Cole [my pastor at that time] preached a stirring message about her life ending with "She is *not*
dead." Then we all stood and sang "Great Is Thy Faithfulness" and watched as dear and precious people filed
past us. We said our goodbys and tearfully watched as
the casket lid was closed upon her.

My beloved friend, Dr. Samuel H. Sutherland, president
emeritus of Biola University, was one of those present at the
funeral that hot September day. He and the hundreds of
people who crowded into the sanctuary didn't seem to mind
the heat. Dr. Sutherland was so touched by the service that
he wrote Dr. Cole these words:

Dear Dr. Ted,

I have participated in and heard many funeral messages,
but I want to say that your remarks at the funeral of Mrs.
Miller the other day were just about the most inspiring and
most helpful I have ever heard. Everything you said was
designed to encourage and uplift the loved ones and many
friends of Mrs. Miller, who naturally were very sorrowful
at the thought of their loss in her homegoing. I am sure it
was a source of great inspiration and untold comfort, especially to her loved ones. The whole service was one of joy and
triumph. Surely the sting of death had been completely
removed in the minds and hearts of all in attendance.

I had the privilege of meeting Mrs. Miller only once or twice, but she must have been a wonderful person and devoted servant of our Lord, because of the influence she had in the life of her beloved husband and the wonderful product that she raised up in the person of our lovely Joyce. Her loved ones, with one accord, rise up and call her blessed.

Again, let me thank you for the inspiration of that hour.

As I read Dr. Sutherland's words, especially "the inspiration of that hour," I thought about the beauty of that day and in all that happened at that funeral. The song I was hearing was definitely one of mourning, but with words like "Great Is Thy Faithfulness" ringing in my ears I could not be totally bogged down in sadness.

The day after my mother's funeral most people went back to their own worlds and concerned themselves with their own affairs. That's as it should be. But I was not one bit prepared to go back to my own world, nor had I anticipated the after-funeral blues. The business of getting on with life has to begin for us who have to deal with our grief, but like everyone who has ever faced the day-after-day-after funeral depression, I was to realize that going on with life was no easy or quick accomplishment.

As I've previously stated, most Christians remember to pray for the grieving family for only about two to three weeks. Within a month the bereaved begin to feel strangely alone. A month after my mother died I found myself staring out my sliding glass doors, overwhelmed with the grief. *What is the matter with me?* I wondered.

I grabbed a pen and wrote down:

Lord, why is it true that always in these moments,
These quiet times and places
I think of them?

Those I have tearfully returned to You.
I think, this morning, I shall die without them.
I'd love to answer the phone and hear her say,
"Hi darling daughter, what's the Lord done for you today?"

Oh, I know she's with You and very much alive,
But that's just the main point of my problem, Lord.
She's with You . . . and not here with me.

Or what about our son?
If he had stayed with us I might be taking him to
    nursery school,
Or picking up a fun assortment of his toys,
Or baking his favorite cookies.
Even KNOWING that You treat them tenderly doesn't
    help much.
I miss them all.
Sometimes I wish You'd hurry and come back so there
    could be
An end to these quiet times and places.

Your sweet, gifted Psalmist lost his son, too . . .
Yet he spoke of being still and knowing You are God.
Was his heart shredding like mine in lonely grief?
Maybe in his quiet place that was the real message.

When I am still and
Knowing You
I am close to them.
Perhaps that's why I am filled with thoughts of them.

Thank you for pivoting my heart from lonely longings to
Your peace,
Your comfort and even a momentary measure of Your joy.

Yet—at these quiet times—
And places
I ache to see them and
I do not understand why I feel so alone
And am grieving so—

Why did I grieve so? Didn't I know my loved ones were
with the Lord? Didn't I know Grandpa was there in heaven,
probably bouncing my little David on his knee? Didn't I know
Mother was proudly showing off her grandson? Didn't I
know they were all safe and happy with the Lord?

Yes, I suppose I did, but that business of being made in
two parts that C. S. Lewis wrote about was becoming a major
reality to me. I responded with my God-side to where my
loved ones were, what they were doing, and who they were
with, but I couldn't seem to get a handle on my human side.
Coping with the daily-ness of life, the loneliness I felt closed
in on me like a cold, dreadful, gray fog.

Many bereaved have experienced this loneliness caused by
the loss of prayers. My friend Ann told of the hundreds of
people who prayed for and sustained her and her husband
during the first weeks after the tragic death of their thirteen-
year-old son. She said, "But just as we felt and experienced
the prayers of all those people in the first week of our son's
death, we just as surely knew when they all *stopped* praying
some weeks later."

It seems when the initial paralyzing shock begins to wear
off, we who are bereaved gradually return to consciousness
like a person coming out of a coma. Senses and feelings return
slowly and sporadically, but mingled in with the good vibra-

tions of being alive and alert again is the scary pain of reality. Precisely at this time our friends, assuming that we the
bereaved are doing just fine, stop praying, stop calling, and
stop doing all those kind, little things that helped so much.

Somehow we need to reverse this trend. In fact, we must
be aware that we may need to hold the bereaved person up to
the Lord more during the first two years of grief than in the
first two weeks. This poem describes the importance of that
support.

Friends

O precious friends, who hold me up
In prayer, I could not drain my cup,
I could not walk this thorny road
Did you not plead for me to God!

How sweet and strange this gift of prayer!
You know my need and voice my care
And speak for me before His throne;
He reaches down, that Holy One,

To smooth the road before my feet;
And thus the circle is complete!
Dear friends of mine, I never knew
That I would owe so much to you!

Martha Snell Nicholson

The song of grief will consume at least two years of our
lives, and sometimes because of circumstances, such as mur-
der or suicide, the song needs to be played for *many* heavy
years. But generally it seems that two birthdays, two Christmas holidays, and two family vacations have to pass before
we begin to adjust to the empty place at the table or the empty
room at the end of the hall. And as the poem goes:

Dear friends of mine, I never knew
That I would owe so much to you!

When my friends Carol and Pete's seventeen-year-old son, Mike, was killed in a car accident, I made a personal commitment to pray for them and their family for at least one year. As I was writing this book in the '70s, the first year after Mike's death had just passed. At that point I received this revealing and remarkable letter from his mother:

Dear Joyce,

Thanks so much for remembering us with the lovely card and then for your faithfulness in prayer for me and my family this past year.

I know it was those prayers that made the difference between something to be only endured or something we and others could learn from. When you are overcome with grief there is a danger of depression, bitterness or even disillusionment with God to creep in. I felt these thoughts and emotions at the door. But they never got in and took hold, because of the power of God there.

Instead there is a new appreciation of what the Resurrection Power really means. That same power that will raise Mike's lifeless body dwells in me now to keep me going. There is a new longing for my Heavenly Home. And there is a new concern for the use of the time given us on earth.

Most psychologists call this one- to two-year period the time when "grief work" is accomplished. The song of grief's work is important to hear and understand if we the bereaved are ever to pick up the pieces of our lives and make some sense out of our suffering. It seems to be written in three parts. At first there is that all-shattering, all-consuming shock that envelopes our whole being when we receive news of a death. This is followed a month or so later by intense suffering and heightened loneliness. Finally, at some point during the first or second year a gradual healing of the mind, soul, and emotions begins to ease us into a kind of acceptance and closure (unless the body is not found or ever recovered—then we tend to stay locked in the second stage).

Based on my own personal experience, I believe that the following are a few of the reasons for listening closely, even though it's difficult, to the lyrics and melody of grief's work song.

We Need the Tears of Grief

Following the shock of hearing that someone has died comes the stress of that information. We need some type of release, and crying is one of the best emotional releases around. To keep our tears locked up in some dark inner space is to suppress our grief, which can only compound our emotional pain later on.

I knew a woman whose thirteen-year-old daughter died suddenly of a brain hemorrhage. The woman went to her daughter's funeral with a peaceful smile on her face. Not once did she lose her composure. Most of the people at the funeral thought it was so wonderful because the woman was taking it so well. "She never cried a single tear," they said of her. I worried about her, and my fears for her mental health were justified six months later when she suffered a tragic mental breakdown and was hospitalized for a very long time. I'm not saying that if you don't cry at a loved one's funeral you'll end up being hospitalized, I'm only saying that crying, if we *can* cry, helps to relieve the tensions of grief.

Somewhere in our Christian culture we're taught that Christians, with the hope of heaven in our hearts, don't cry. But we must not be ashamed of our tears. Jesus wept on hearing of his friend Lazarus's death, even though he knew he was about to return Lazarus to life. To weep over the death of a loved one is not a sign that we are guilty of having little or no faith, nor is it a sign of hopelessness. Crying is a natural part of being human and is never needed more than in the grieving process.

A widow told me about a woman who was the main speaker for a women's retreat. She said that the speaker, a widow herself, talked of having *no* tears or grief when her husband died. The woman said that God was an all-purpose God: therefore, she did not grieve or weep.

The women in her audience who were widows listened in stunned agony. Their reaction was twofold and united: They were hurt and angry. They talked of the experience, in their rooms after the meeting had ended. They all asked the same questions:

> "Why didn't God do that for me?"
>
> "How come I can't stop crying, and why do I fall apart so easily?"
>
> "Am I guilty of committing some sin, or am I lacking in faith so much that God doesn't take away *my* tears?"
>
> "If God did this special act of loving grace for her, why didn't he do it for me?"

I don't doubt that the conference speaker was sincere. I'm also sure the woman was truthful when she said she did not shed any tears after her husband's death. But besides not being sensitive to the widows in her audience, she herself missed the beautiful melody that the song of tears would have brought to her.

We know from Revelation 7:17 and 21:4 that when we get to heaven God will wipe away our tears. But what of now? I believe that God did a good thing when he gave us the ability to cry. Think of it: For us who are here on this earth, for the time of our deepest sorrow, God has designed us with a valve that can give us some temporary relief from the pressure of our burdened hearts while we are healing.

Have you ever wondered why the Bible in Romans 12:15 states that we must weep with those who weep? I believe that practice to be of equal benefit to the bereaved and to the friend who weeps with them. It's a beautiful bonding process and comforts more than any word or other action.

The value of tears and of weeping with those who weep was articulately described in the following letter by a father and mother who had lost their three-year-old son. Notice how many times they were comforted by the ministry of others' tears at the time of his death. Their words were printed in the newsletter of the First Baptist Church of Fullerton, California.

A Letter to the Church Family

Our Dear Friends:

We thank you for being real with emotions; no one can be strong about death. There is a special language for moments like these. However, it can't be written. It is expressed only through the embraces, tears, and compassion of loving people.

Our beautiful child died, and we don't understand why. We ached, bled, and wept. We hurt so that our own survival seemed impossible. The awful depression numbed our bodies, and our thoughts screamed out of control that it was all an ugly dream.

If we had been asked off the cuff before the tragedy, in one of those meaningless philosophical discussions that now seem so empty, we might have chosen solitude for a time like Thursday evening. BUT PEOPLE CAME. There were no meaningless words, only broken hearts, embraces, and love. Our hearts were broken and so were those of our precious friends.

On Thursday night we learned the value of intruding upon the hurting. We were not left alone in our grief. People with wet faces and eager, grabbing hearts broke down the facades we had created and gave their love.

The small groups of which we had been a part saved Sue and me. The groups of friends with whom we met to pray and share were like our own torn flesh. Because we had shared so much before, they immediately reached and took those chances we always have a hard time taking (total involvement). They touched our faces, embraced and held our weary bodies, and shared our wounded souls.

But, compassion has no age. A group of young people came to us. Young people with whom Sue and I had laughed, cried, and loved. This time we needed them. They had not been taught to share in the agony of death. They were really afraid to come. But, they did come. And, they held us and wept with us. We were overcome by their love and compassion. They loved, shared, wept unashamedly.

But, the group grew larger. The walls of an institution we had worked to change, fell. People reached, reached, reached, and we needed and wanted them. Each person that came was ripped and angered and crushed with us. We felt it!

Christ's love came in all those people who pushed us back into the terrible reality, and bandaged us with hope and love. We love you all.

And you, our dear friends, Emory and Loeta [the pastor and his wife]. You gave us new life when we wanted only death. You gave hope and life and the reality of going on. How do you do it? God gave you a gift that others need so deeply. You are so tender and loving. I told Sue you were exact. You did and said the perfect things. How can we ever, ever thank you? The service was just as we wanted it with favorite memories of our son and our hope. Oh God, how we loved our little Joel. The hurt will never really stop. But you, the tender people of our church, helped so much.

We're moving to a new city. We're not running away. Our plans had been made before, and we feel it best to carry them out now. Come see us. Invite us to your homes. Don't hesitate to share with us your memories of Joel. They are so precious to us, and how we appreciate those of you who took time to care for, share, and love our little guy.

How can we thank each of you for your love? It has simply seen us through this time. Please know this. One thing we have surely learned is that "words of comfort" are nonexistent. No one has magic words. Yet there is a comfort through your clasping, embracing, and sobbing with us. We can't adequately thank you for coming to our homes, and to Joel's memorial service. For we have learned above all things that God's love comes through people.

Love,

Walt & Sue Buster

and all our family who were overwhelmed by your love.

This letter was followed by a beautiful statement from the pastor, the Reverend Emory C. Campbell. It said:

The foregoing letter from Walt and Sue Buster expresses beautifully what the church really is about. When I received word on Thursday night of the tragic death of little Joel Buster I was at Thousand Pines with our Jr. High Camp. By the time I drove down the mountain, our church family had surrounded them with love. It is so good that God has given us the capacity to cry when we hurt and to cry with others when they hurt.

Of the church St. Paul said truly, "If one part suffers, all parts suffer with it." We are one in the Spirit and thus we feel deeply with each other.

Love and joy to you all,
Emory C. Campbell

The capacity to cry when we hurt and to weep with others when they hurt is one of the most touching ways to carry out the scriptural admonition to "bear ye one another's burdens." We must develop our capacity to cry. I know a marvelous minister who was aware of this need in his life and prayed for "the ministry of tears" to be developed in his heart. God answered his prayer. Since that prayer his overall ministry has taken on a new depth and dimension. In times of bereavement we need the release of tears to wash away the gray tensions of our soul; and when tears come, they do not require an apology or explanation.

Weeping with someone is often best done while holding the hands of the brokenhearted. We also need to reach out, and even if briefly, physically embrace the bereaved. In the preceding letter the line, "They touched our faces, embraced and held our weary bodies and shared our wounded souls" tells of the exceptional value of combining tears of understanding with tender, wordless embraces. Our first worry always seems to be about what we will *say* to the bereaved.

Yet a handclasp, a quick hug, or a small touch on the shoulder can say a world of words and say it in silence.

We Need the Slowness of Grief

Time feels like it has come to a complete stop after we lose a loved one. The most unbearable stretch of each day seems to be those dark hours just before daybreak. We don't feel free to call our friends or pastor at four in the morning, so we feel acutely alone. It's cold, dark, and so forbidding at that time of day that our anxiety gets thick enough to cut with a knife.

We must not become impatient with the slowness of grief's music, however. Its *largo* tempo (which plods along at a maddeningly slow pace) may be very essential in God's plan for our more healthy recovery. We struggle with this rhythm and long for the upbeat tempo of what we recognize as "normal" for our life's melody. But it may take what feels like an eternity before the finale of our grief's song.

Since my son David was the first of anyone close to me to die, I had no idea at that time that working through my grief would be a plodding, faltering process. One afternoon I blurted out to a friend, "I don't understand why I'm still crying or why this hurts so much. After all, it's been two whole weeks since David died." Months later I grew even more impatient with myself. I raked my soul over the coals and told myself that I was being very immature over all of this. Somehow I had the idea that grieving and crying more than a week or so was a sign of weakness. The thought that I might be right on schedule in a very normal timetable never occurred to me.

Over the years I've learned that if we rush this time of adjusting, we rob grief of the work it needs to do. We must try not to be hard on ourselves or in such a hurry to get our lives or those of our bereaved friends "back to normal." It is essential for us to remember that *normal* has been forever altered into *abnormal.*

Recently as I went through six months of chemo treatments I felt as if each day was a year long. And now that I am six months past chemo I am remembering my own words here: *normal* even now has been forever altered.

If we are not allowed to grieve, another problem is created: guilt. We who walk away from a grave site do not want to bring down a mental curtain, shutting off forever our loved one who has died. Leaving them, walking away and forgetting them is unthinkably cruel. In the very least it seems to be disloyal. To walk away and in effect dismiss them from our lives causes a guilty feeling in us, as if we're not being faithful or loyal to the deceased. We need to give the grieving person the time he or she needs.

The bereaved must be encouraged to talk and to express their feelings, whether they be sad, angry, or lonely. When I experienced my losses, I desperately wanted to talk with someone about death, but hardly anyone would talk about it with me. Instead, people gave me some rather sticky-sweet, pie-in-the-sky-by-and-by books that depressed me even more. At that point, what I needed was not books, but people: warm flesh and blood; people who would listen to me as I poured out my grief, my questions, and my regrets.

Most of the books told me I should not be sad about losing my loved one because I was a Christian with hope. My loved one was with the Lord, and that was supposed to make everything go rushing back to "normal" in my heart. What I didn't understand was, if that were true about my Christianity and hope, how come I *was sad;* a totally depressed kind of sad?

What I wish I'd known then is that the desperate sadness of grief would be with me for a good long while. I think it would have helped me in my grieving process had I known that the slowness of grief would give me the perfect opportunity to express my sorrow, to lay it out on the table before me so I could begin to deal with it.

Eventually I did heal emotionally, and I did see the lovely hope of God. But in the years after David's, my grandfather's, and my mother's deaths, to hear or read "Buck up, life isn't quite all *that* bad—after all, you're a Christian!" was an unbelievable blow and a frustration quite beyond my comprehension.

If you have just lost your husband, wife, child, or friend, acknowledge the much-needed work of the slowness of grief. I pray that understanding will help ease the pain, fear, and dread of this time. I found that it helped me to memorize this verse from John where Jesus says: "No, I will not abandon you or leave you as orphans in the storm, I will come to you" (John 14:18). If just before dawn, when the hours are at their darkest, you and I can repeat those beautifully honest words, the tempo of grief will not seem so slow. We will be better able to wait the storm out.

We Need to Accept the Lethargy of Grief

For someone who has always been a bundle of energy, always on the go, full of drive, or as they used to say, full of "pep and vinegar," the lethargy of grief is an arduous, toilsome mental frustration. It is difficult, if not almost impossible, to decipher the change in our normal, routine methods and attitudes.

The lethargy of grief strikes a normally decisive person, and he or she finds it takes a superhuman amount of effort to make even the smallest choice. A woman discovers in the first few months of her widowhood she does not have the strength, will, or remotest desire at 5:30 P.M. to choose between mashed potatoes or baked potatoes. It all seems so useless to decide on *anything*. As I dealt with chemo treatments for my cancer a few months ago, I remembered how making decisions confused me, and with that confusion came an overwhelming sense of frustration.

C. S. Lewis describes this lethargy as the "laziness of grief." I saw a vivid example of the lethargy or "laziness" of grief a month or two after my mother died. I'd driven over to my father's home to visit with him and was appalled at the utter chaos of his house. He and my sister were the only two people living there, yet the house looked as if several families were co-existing there, all jammed together.

It was when I started to clean the house, to try to put it into some semblance of order, that I discovered the main reason for the mess. Everywhere I looked in each room I entered, there were stacks of opened mail. Evidently my father had received even more correspondence than usual. Each day he'd opened it wherever he happened to be, read it, and then laid it down where he had been standing.

There were stacks of mail in the usual place on the kitchen desk, but also on the stove, the refrigerator, and on top of the washer. Correspondence, bills, and sympathy cards were stuck in between the wooden dowels of the front hall room dividers; piles of opened mail were all over the bedrooms and the den; there was not a table, chair, or couch in the living room without some bits and pieces of opened mail. Even both bathrooms had not escaped the landslide of litter.

In putting sense to all this, I realized my father had lost his wife of thirty-seven years, and with that loss his interest in going on with his life had been destroyed. Dad's curiosity about the contents of the mail helped him open it, but the lethargy of grief stole his drive and zest for living so that he simply laid down the opened envelopes wherever he was in the house. Responding to the mail in any way did not occur to him.

We must understand that when death hits us it will completely disrupt our entire life schedule. "Oh, what's the use?" will be our most continual thought. But lethargy, like the slowness of grief, is a temporary phenomenon. After the first

anguishing shock of death has subsided a bit, the bereaved
will need special attention, love, and support, because this
period of lethargy is so subtle they hardly know it's happening. Like my father, they may not be aware of it at all.

This is *not* the moment for friends to ask, "Is there anything I can do?" This is a time for friends to recognize the
lethargy as normal and to be sensitive to the work that lethargy
is trying to accomplish. When the bereaved is ready to resume
normal social functions, family relationships, or daily employ-
ment, friends can help the transition by *doing*, not asking.

My journal entries written soon after David died reveal my
mental and emotional adjustment to the lethargic time of my
grief:

*In the past months of pregnancy, I've never been so ill.
Now I am recovering from both that illness and David's
death. Every time I turn around I hear someone say, "If
there's anything I can do, just let me know." I just smile
and say, "No, thank you." Actually there's much to be done,
but somehow I simply don't want to do anything and
wouldn't dream of asking anyone else to.*

In fairness, I must say that during that time some of my
caring friends did come to the rescue. They understood,
somehow, about my lethargy and didn't ask if they could
help—they just helped! There was a young woman, Andrea,
home from college for Christmas, who said, "Joyce, when
you want the children out of the house for a while, I'll come
over and pick them up." Another college-aged woman,
Glenda, said, "It's the day before Christmas and I'm free.
Which do you want me to do, the dusting or the ironing?"
(She ironed.) My friend Eleanor phoned and said, "I'm fix-
ing dinner for your family one night this week. Which night
would be best?" My friend Shirley simply shoved a cake into

Laurie's hands at the front door and said, "Tell your mother this is from me." Dorothy, my minister's wife, one of the busiest women I knew, phoned to say, "I've just baked two lemon pies. Would it be convenient for me to bring them over now?" My friend and co-worker Al Sanders, founder of Ambassador Advertising, said, "On Monday I'm sending Ginger [his personal secretary] over for the day to help you take care of your mail." And Margaret, Al's wife, sent a large beef roast along with Ginger.

Jane Huff, in her book *Whom the Lord Loveth,* said that after a long illness of hers she knew what to do for people in need! A friend asked Jane what was the first thing she would do for a sick person. Jane's instantaneous answer was, "The dishes!"

The bereaved need to be surrounded by such friends who do the dishes and whose actions are motivated by Paul's words in Ephesians 5:15–17:

> So be careful how you act; these are difficult days. Don't
> be fools; be wise; make the most of every opportunity
> you have for doing good. Don't act thoughtlessly, but
> try to find out and do whatever the Lord wants you to.

I believe that the secret is to ask the Lord what we as friends can do and then go do it in his name. We can be of enormous help during this temporary lethargy in a grieving person's progress toward wholeness and the healing of their grief.

We Need to Know the Humility of Grief

The intense pain of grief has a unique way of leveling our pride, and I believe it produces a humility which can enlarge our growth of character. The music of this portion of grief's song is not terribly pleasant or soothing, but then real growth is never soothing, especially while it's happening. It generally hurts to grow. I wish that were not true, but it seems any experience which forces us into growth will be accompanied by its own high-priced agony.

My physical growth as a child was quite an ordeal as I generally managed to catch every germ and disease that came along. Most of the time my companions were flu, colds, and bronchitis. Those years of being ill developed some unique resources in me, however. For instance, long days in bed with illness gave me an opportunity to learn to be alone without being lonely. I took lessons in how to fill up my time while being confined—in fact, that's when I discovered the joy of reading books. Another one of the side effects of so many illnesses was that I developed an empathy toward others who were sick. My capacity to care took shape and enlarged under the humbling experiences of being sick.

Today when I hear people brag, "I've never been sick a day in my whole life," I feel a tad sorry for them in a way, because pain and illness can produce a rare quality of aliveness within our souls like nothing else can. That boastful statement also suggests to me that when they *do* get sick, as they probably will, they will have a difficult time coping with the onset of pain and depression.

Pastor Ted Cole, told of grief working humility in his father. Rolland Cole was a strong, healthy, robust man, six-feet four-inches tall, weighing 250 pounds. He was hardly ever sick, nor had he ever had many health problems. There wasn't too much he felt he couldn't handle. Then, in his sixties, cancer moved in and began to take over the cells in the big man's body. Months later, as dying became imminent, Dr. Ted watched with fascination as his dad's character underwent a transformation.

Rolland Cole, once ready to impatiently denounce people or events, began to develop large amounts of Christian grace, love, and patience toward others. The more ill he became and the closer he felt death advancing toward him, the more his pride was leveled. Everyone around him saw a man of humility. He died a beautiful man. We had seen the incredible work of humility blossom in Rolland's life.

We Need to Use Grief as a Creative Gift

As much as we need the tears, the slowness, the lethargy, and the humility of grief, we must not stay in grief for the rest of our lives. We should give those elements enough time to do their work in our lives and then consider our loss in terms of a creative gift.

The famous Tracy Clinic for deaf children was never planned for or even considered until Spencer Tracy and his wife gave birth to a son who was totally deaf. Out of little John's deafness this clinic, one of the finest in the world, was envisioned by his mother, and her dream of a clinic was brought into existence.

In the terrible months of grieving solitude following my mother's death in 1966, I never dreamed I'd find anything creative in dying. But a few years later, I wrote in *The Richest Lady in Town*:

> It should have been the end of her, but then we found all her notebooks: big spiral ones, little spiral ones, date books, secretary pads, loose-leaf binders, and even her diary kept before she met my father. They were a treasure house of ideas, theories, and inspiration—the essence of fifty-seven years of being God's woman.

Over and over again I read and reread those books she left. It was the most creative collection of gifts I've ever seen, and it came straight from God. I've continued to use her material in every book I've written so far. I'll be eternally grateful to Mother that while she was alive she took the time to write down her thoughts, ideas, and many of her prayers. My mother had no plans whatsoever for publishing anything she wrote, yet she is now published. Those notebooks are far more valuable to me than a financial inheritance of *any* amount I could have received from her.

Another person who has used her personal grief as a creative gift to help others is Dale Evans Rogers. It was because

Dale and Roy Rogers lost their precious two-year-old daughter, Robin, that society's attitude and treatment of Down's syndrome children drastically changed. Dale took her grief, used it as a gift, and poured herself into the book *Angel Unaware*.

Because she was willing to be open and honest about Robin she was able to use her grief as a creative gift. Through that book Dale threw open the doors of thousands of homes. Families who had previously hidden their retarded children in the dark shadows of their private lives, sometimes not telling even their families about them, began to come forward, and best of all, began to accept God's gentle healing. Down's syndrome children were no longer treated as people to be shunned and avoided, after Dale shared her poignant story.

Dr. Norman Vincent Peale wrote of Dale in *Angel Unaware*:

> She is a mother who has won great victory over great sorrow. . . . I saw at once that Robin, her baby, had not lived and died in vain. Where most babies die and leave the mother crushed, Robin put on immortality and her mother found the very joy of God in what might otherwise have been an overwhelming tragedy.

That book was only the beginning of Dale's using grief as a creative gift. In the decades that followed the publication of Robin's story Dale has lost several other children, and the rich store of books that have flowed from her pen have become a scintillating, freeing ministry to millions of people.

After the loss of my infant son David, one of Dale's books reached out to me at precisely the moment it was needed. It was a new book called *Dearest Debbie*, in which Dale, using her grief again as a gift, penned the story of her daughter Debbie, who had been tragically killed in a bus accident. My mother gave it to me the day the first copy reached California bookstores, and it came none too soon.

My son and daughter, Rick and Laurie, were having a very hard time adjusting to their brother David's death. To us it seemed that just when God promised we'd all have a healthy baby, he was gone. I sat Rick and Laurie down and read aloud Dale's entire book about Debbie.

When I had finished I said, "Now, what do you think that book said to you?" Both Rick, who was twelve, and Laurie, just ten, were crying.

Laurie voiced their identical feelings when tearfully she said, "That book helps me to understand about David dying, and I feel better about him being with God." I breathed a sigh of relief, but then Laurie added, "But don't read it again to me because it's too beautiful-sad." I smiled and promised her I wouldn't reread it, but I could tell that healing had begun in them. And it had been motivated by Dale's willingness to accept her grief as a creative gift to give others.

When you read the introduction to this book, you may not have fully understood my words in describing my own cancer as a "terrible and beautiful gift"; but in this chapter I want to make the point that we should use our grief as a creative gift, and I now intend to practice what I preach. Cancer is a terrible gift because it completely turns one's world upside down and shakes all moorings loose. I have found myself, for all these months now, going through all the grief stages: denial, anger, bargaining, depression, and acceptance. I've also seen in progress the particular grief-work that I've written about in this chapter. But my own words, "We need to use grief as a creative gift," are pounding inside me and demanding to be heard.

I wonder how long I'll have this terrible gift—three years? thirty years? Or will I die from some unrelated disease or from a different cancer in a new location? I don't know the answers to these questions. None of us do. But I think cancer has forced me to deal with the question of not how long do I have, but what will I do with whatever time I *do* have? So, as I deal on a daily basis with this life-threatening disease, I can thank God for such a terrible gift, for it certainly clarifies my thoughts about what directions I want to take, as well as about what is utterly frivolous in my life and what is of supreme importance.

Hence, cancer to me is a beautiful gift as well. I've been given a wake-up call; a call to see in a more pristine way the people around me and the people at a distance; a chance, an opportunity if you will, to use whatever time I have left to be what I believe God wants me to be. The gift of cancer affords me many opportunities. So, with God's help and the loving support of my cherished husband, my wonderful family, and my closest friends, I'll endeavor to carry out the mission statement of my life and to do it with as much grace as I can possibly sustain, for as long as I can.

I can hear the song God sang to Joshua when he said, "As I was with Moses, so shall I be with you." I know I'm no Joshua or Moses, but I am, like you, a child of God, so I take great comfort from these words and am able to thank him for his gift.

I have found that if we examine and put into practice these five definite works: the tears, slowness, lethargy, humility, and creativity of grief, it seems to soften the harshness of our mourning song, and sweeping in, the music comes back with its own newborn, majestic splendor. We can never be the same again, and we can bear to listen to the song without breaking apart.

9

The Lasting Song of Restoration

. . . out of His infinite riches in Jesus
He giveth and giveth and giveth again.
Annie Johnson Flint

The work of recovery and restoration is one of the most important elements in our lives after death has taken a loved one away; without it we may never be able to move on with life. We may remain frozen in space, feeling only our bereavement, never feeling well or *whole* again.

Have you ever wondered why at many funerals someone reads the twenty-third psalm? If it's not repeated by the minister, rabbi, or priest, then it's printed for us to read or its message is brought to us in a song. In some manner the poetic beauty of this oft-quoted psalm is brought to our attention. And even in our sadness, its lyricism seems to transcend all racial boundaries, all religious creeds; it is a powerful comfort, no matter who has died.

I believe that the reason for the enormous popularity of the twenty-third psalm down through the years is its enduring ability to help us begin to restore our splintered emo-

199

tions. To me the key word is found early in the psalm in the third verse. Here are some of the translations:

"He restoreth my soul" (KJV).
"He revives my soul" (MLB).
"He restores my failing health" (LB).
"He restores my soul" (RSV).

All that third verse says basically is, "God heals me"; and verse three turns out to be the most important message we could hear in our grief-stricken moments.

Here we are: alone, feeling like we're cut in half, tearful, weary, and heartsick. Then we hear the music of restoration start up. The lyrics come to us as if on angels' wings: "Because the Lord is my Shepherd, I have everything I need! He lets me rest in the meadow grass and leads me beside the quiet streams." Later the words awaken some hidden little place of hope within us with the words: "Even when walking through the dark valley of death I will not be afraid, for you are close beside me, guarding, guiding all the way."

As people who call themselves God's children, we are thrilled that God is bringing the lasting, continuous song of restoration to our being. It's one of the consoling fringe benefits of knowing Christ.

But what of those who have no hope in Christ? What do the magnificent words of the twenty-third psalm do for them except pour oil on a large, gaping, bleeding wound? What about those bereaved souls who can only guess there *may* be a life after death? Or those who come to funerals and hope and pray their loved one has gone to heaven, if there is one?

I remember the first funeral where I observed some mourners who had no hope. They couldn't hear the song of restoration, and their grief could not be comforted. The family of the deceased had arrived at the service on time, but most of them had been drinking. I pulled my pious shirt around me and reacted to their being inebriated in a super-spiritual, absolutely nauseating way. *How crass,* I thought. Rather contemptuously, I mentally denounced their actions as definitely in bad taste.

Within an instant of my judgmental attitude, God, with one destructive blow to my self-righteous pride, brought me to a new state of humility and compassion. In my mind I could hear him admonishing me. *Joyce, why are you so filled with such righteous indignation? Why are you so quick to criticize their behavior? Don't you realize they are sorrowing with no hope? I know them, but they don't know me. They don't know I've come to give eternal life, and they don't know that there is more—they think this life is all there is. Don't be angry with them because they have tried to escape death's ugly reality by drinking. You need to give them grace and understanding. After all, what else do they have to turn to?*

With a much softened heart I looked again at the grieving family of the man in the casket, and even though my compassion was newly acquired, I could feel for them. I could understand that people without faith, without forgiveness, and without God's comforting peace come to funerals to say a forever good-bye. They don't come to whisper, "I'll see you in the morning." They don't know if there is a morning. Death comes to their lives as the finale, the final departure; and certainly to their thinking no psalm, even the twenty-third, is going to put things right again for them. It is easier for these loved ones to bear the funeral if their senses are not exposed to the raw, naked hurt of death. So they come to mourn, hoping their senses will be numbed enough so they will hardly see, hear, or feel.

What a difference for anyone who knows the Lord: Not only is living transformed, but so is dying! It's a brand-new ball game altogether for Christians. If we believe what Jesus taught, then we are not left hopeless when a loved one dies. We are not left with only these brief days on earth, but amazingly, we have gained eternity. We do not have to vaguely fantasize about the possibility of reincarnation, or whether or not there is life after death. Our faith in Christ assures us by giving us positive answers.

Hence, when we who love the Lord do sorrow, it is this hope of God that will not let us sorrow in finality and defeat. We are not abandoned to the lonely struggle of living alone in our frustrating grief. In short, our hope in Christ and living with Him after death *is* our song of restoration.

Paul never said it better or more clearly than when he wrote to the church at Thessalonica:

> And now, dear brothers, I want you to know what happens to a Christian when he dies so that when it happens, you will not be full of sorrow, as those are who have no hope. For since we believe that Jesus died and then came back to life again, we can also believe that when Jesus returns, God will bring back with him all the Christians who have died.
>
> 1 Thessalonians 4:13–14

Every time I've seen those two verses lately I think of Mary Ann, a lady who belonged to my church. After her death, her husband—grieving terribly, yes, but not without hope—wrote this letter to the Sunday school class they had attended. Bob ended the letter by referring to these marvelous words of Paul.

Dear Chapel Class Friends:

These flowers are in a small way in appreciation for your Christian love and kindness and gifts of food for me and my family during a time of life's greatest sorrow—to lose a lovely wife and Mother.

Mary Ann loved each of you and was heartbroken when she could no longer attend class due to her poor health. She was so thrilled with the special recording of the class music and message that she had me play it over and over for her.

We thank you from the bottom of our hearts for the love
and joy you brought to her in this manner.

Please be comforted in knowing that Mary Ann believed
in the saving blood of Jesus Christ, and that she prayed for
the members of the Chapel Class at each opportunity, asking God's richest blessings upon each of you. She prayed also
that the Lord Jesus Christ would take her home to be with
Him, for she believed to be absent from the body is to be present with the Lord in Heaven.

Although we shall grieve the loss of Mary Ann, and there
will be a great void in our lives, we are comforted by God's
Holy Word when we read 1 Thessalonians 4:13-18.

Yours in Christian Love,

Bob Edwards

In my own life, back in the '60s when God wanted to
restore my heart with his hope, he allowed me to find a very
explicit explanation, in my mother's handwriting, of that
hope. Among her many notebooks and papers I found a pen-
ciled, rough-draft copy of a letter she had written about six
months before her death to her dear friend Esther. Here, set
down so accurately, is the picture of death when it comes to
Christians. Mother had written:

My dear Esther,

In the recent death of your dear mother these few lines
of encouragement are easy to write to you because you have
had the experience of rebirth and you belong to the King-
dom of God. You know, in a vital, personal way that you
are one of God's little children and you also know that this

human existence is but the first act to our spiritual (real) existence.

Belief in Christ and His immortality gives us the moral strength and the guidance we need for virtually every action in our daily lives. When you came in contact with Christ you received eternal life. The Word of God teaches us—and strengthens our belief in the continuity of our spiritual existence after death.

We live for a very short time in our natural bodies, but we live eternally in our spiritual bodies. So the passing on, plainly spoken, the death of your dear mother is in reality a continuation of her existence in what is now her spiritual body. Her human body died. That body was no longer strong enough for her to use it any more. But Esther, your mother did not die—only her body did! St. Paul says, as there's a natural body, so will there be a spiritual body.

It is wonderful to know (and believe) that we shall know one another just as we know our loved ones here on earth.

I know you have had a terrible loss and heartache. The breaking of human ties and the closing of earthly chapters in our lives brings sorrow and pain, but healing comes to us when we accept the reality of death and dying. Healing comes, too, when we realize that our life continues in another form more glorious than the human mind can imagine!

In trying to sort all this grief and troubled times out in your life, let us admit frankly that we are entering a realm of faith. Since no one has returned to tell us what lies on the other side, we must go on living by faith. Faith in the existence of God and faith by the teachings of Jesus Christ.

Death, then, is not merely a solemn, dark curtain, rung down on the first act of the stage of this all too brief earthly life, but it is the lifting of the curtain on the most wonderful and final act of life's drama. We are passed from death unto life!

Your life, dear Esther, is a blessing to many so may this recent experience show that life's greatest achievement, in the long run, is to know and have peace with God.

My prayer is for God to give you strength for your immediate needs.

In the bond of Christian love,

Marion

I believe God has made a special provision for those who are with him to be able to look down and see us who have been left behind. I also believe, strange as it may sound to you, that God makes those dear, departed loved ones angels who, by one way or another, minister back here on earth to us in times of our need.

I believe my mother probably saw me as, almost a year after her death, I found her letter to Esther; and she smiled because she knew I'd be restored by reading it. She also probably saw that wherever she had written the name *Esther* in the letter I had inserted *Joyce.* Finding her papers enabled me to see the work of restoration begin to blossom in my life.

Since I also believe that the dead in Christ are with him (alive and active) and can observe our lives here, I have no doubt my mother is well aware of my struggle with cancer. I feel certain too, that because they who are with the Lord know all about the ending passages and have come through the dying process, they are not worried or filled with anxiety as they watch us in our struggles. No, it's far different from that. Right now, my mother's presence is as real and pungent as a summer bouquet of flowers, and I can feel her urging me on to finish the race here, to give it my best, to serve the Lord with all my heart for whatever time there is. And I am deeply comforted by her reassuring presence.

As well as I can understand it, God does his remarkable work of restoration in our hearts by three methods. It is my hope—no, my prayer—that you will allow God to help you open your mind, your emotions, and your will to receive him and his song of restoration. The last thing in the world I want to do is smugly pat you on the back and tell you "Time heals all wounds" or "Everything is coming up roses" or parrot the phrase, "Isn't it nice your loved one is with the Lord?" But I know for a fact that *God does restore our souls and we can recuperate* from our devastating losses if we are wise enough to open our ears and our hearts to hear the inspiring melody of God's mourning song.

Forgiveness

The first faint strains of restoration's song begin with forgiveness. I doubt that anything can be done for us in our grief, whether we are grieving for ourselves, as I am with aggressive cancer, or for someone's death, unless we begin with a concept of forgiveness. For the Christian entwined with death or dying, forgiveness may well start with forgiving—surprise!—God.

You and I may have our time of angrily demanding of God the whys of our problem as my mother did when she gave the Lord a mental tongue-lashing over Dr. Carlson's death; but healing, hope, and acceptance of death will not come until we forgive God for allowing this thing or this death to happen.

I spoke at a luncheon while I was working on this manuscript in the '70s. A woman heard my brief remarks about this book as I shared some of the lessons I'd learned about the mourning song. At the close of the luncheon, although she had no idea I'd be writing this chapter about forgiveness, she felt impressed by God to share her personal story with me. I'm grateful because she told me about her inward reactions to losing her darling, beloved grandson.

She said that in the beginning there was no way she could accept the little boy's death. She felt angry toward God and could not come up with any reason why this beautiful child had to die. The more she thought about it, the madder she got; and one day, as loud and clear as a human voice would sound, she heard the Lord say within her heart, *Will you forgive me for his death?*

At first she was stunned by his amazing question. God was asking her for forgiveness? Slowly, she realized she had been accusing and blaming God for her grandson's death. She related to me that almost as soon as she had answered the Lord's question with a yes, the peace of God gently slipped into the vacant spot in her heart, and she experienced a healing of her spirit.

In a letter to my brother, Cliff, a few months before she died, my mother documented the fact that she had forgiven God for his direction and handling of her life's course. She wrote:

I thank God for the joy and peace I have in my heart made possible by Him.

Tomorrow I go to UCLA again, but I am not afraid and I thank God that Christ is with me.

My son, God has a chartered course for all of us. He whispered so sweetly to me a few weeks ago that if I put Him first in my life—He'll see that I come in second.

So I put myself in His care. Now I've asked Him to pilot the course laid out for me and for my dear family.

God bless you, Son. You will face hard, trying days; but I know you'll come through with flying colors.

Be not afraid neither be dismayed for the Lord God is with you wherever you go.

Lovingly,
Mother

She wanted my brother and all her family to know that she had forgiven God for the "chartered course" he'd obviously begun plotting for her. That is exactly why she started the letter with thanks to God. Then she made sure that we knew of her conversation with the Lord so we'd know it was all right between them. Her forgiveness of God was up to date.

I think she also wanted us to know that even when we didn't see any evidence of God caring or working in our lives, we were to trust him and take whatever tiny amount of faith we had and remember that God and his loving promises could be trusted. The pilot would not run our ship aground or dash us against the rocky reefs. Mother ended her letter with the added admonition for Cliff not only to remember God's promises, but also to remember them *without fear*, no matter how trying the days might become.

Not only did we, as her family, understand my mother had forgiven God for her breast and lung cancer, but her friends knew as well. After my mother's death, a letter received from Jeanne, a dear friend of the Miller family, read in part:

About your mother's death, my mind did a flashback of two scenes.

One: The first time I met your parents at the little old musty smelling synagogue in Reseda that your dad rented to start his little church until the sanctuary was built, and from which I went representing them as their first missionary to a foreign land.

Two: Several years later as I stood with both your mom and dad, holding hands and forming a circle for prayer in their living room. Even though your mom was up, she was unable to go out anymore. Her prayer (I can still feel even though she was well aware of her condition) was beautiful and with her gentle words she melted my very soul. She drew us all nearer that day to the Christ she was soon to meet. That was the last time I saw her . . . here.

I wonder if my mother's prayer that day would have drawn Jeanne closer to the Lord had it not been for the song of forgiveness in Mother's heart? I don't think so.

My sister, Marilyn, who was fourteen at the time of Mother's death, had to deal with forgiving God, too. I described the start of restoration's song in Marilyn's heart in *The Richest Lady in Town*:

It was just hours after our mother's funeral. Marilyn was fourteen, frightened, and unbelievably hurt and bewildered by Mother's death.

Friends and relatives had left. I'd gone home with my family; my brother, Cliff, had taken a military jet back to Vietnam, and my father had wearily gone to bed.

Marilyn went into the den and, realizing her aloneness, asked God to be her Friend, Savior, and Comforter. In short, she did an incredible thing: *she forgave the Lord for taking her mother.* God, in turn, melted the hurt and bitterness and began to heal her torn heart. In those moments she started to become the beautiful, wealthy person we love.

When I think of Marilyn, at such a young age forgiving the Lord for Mother's death, I remember the widow who said angrily to me, "Just how am I supposed to be thankful for my husband's death two years ago?"

I told her I didn't think she'd *ever* get over that death until she could get to the bottom of the problem. There she stood, some two years after her husband's death, still shaking her fist in God's face demanding to know why He had done this terrible thing to her. I fear all of us will always be spiritually poor until the lesson of forgiveness melts our hardened heart and begins its healing.

Marilyn is rich because her forgiveness is up to date. She's determined to be the woman God wants her to be.

In addition to forgiving God, we need to forgive ourselves. Very often, in the days following the loss of a loved one we pile up a huge stack of regrets. We remember each thing we did (or did not do) with the deceased; we relive old conversations and conflicts. We dredge up everything in our past that we wish we had done, and we struggle daily with those remorseful feelings.

Martha Snell Nicholson, herself an invalid for over twenty-five years, said it best when she wrote this poem:

Remembered Sin

I made a lash of my remembered sins.
I wove it firm and strong, with cruel tip,
And though my quivering flesh shrank from the scourge,
With steady arm I plied the ruthless whip.

For surely I, who had betrayed my Lord,
Must needs endure this sting of memory.
But though my stripes grew sore, there came no peace.
And so I looked again to Calvary.

His tender eyes beneath the crown of thorns
Met mine; His sweet voice said, "My child, although
Those oft-remembered sins of thine have been
Like crimson, scarlet, they are now like snow.

"My blood, shed here, has washed them all away,
And there remaineth not the least dark spot,
Nor any memory of them; and so
Should you remember sins which God forgot?"

I stood there trembling, bathed in light, though scarce
My tired heart dared to hope. His voice went on:
"Look at thy feet, My child." I looked, and lo,
The whip of my remembered sins was gone!

I'm sure God longs to take away our whips of remembered sins. And Martha's question is extremely important: "Should you remember sins which God forgot?" If the painful slashes on our souls are ever to heal, we need to forgive ourselves as God has forgiven us. We need to deliberately dwell on the comforting thought that when God *forgave* those sins and regrets he *forgot* them as well. Forgetting, for us humans, is a whole lot harder than forgiving.

After we have forgiven God and ourselves, we may need to forgive other people. Fortunately, we are not asked to forget in order to be able to forgive.

The healing that followed forgiveness in my own life came after I forgave God for the death of my son David and then forgave (with God's help) my parents for missing David's memorial service. I've already related that until I put my regrets and angers into God's hands, I couldn't get well— not physically, nor in my heart and spirit. When we can surrender people, places, and painful events into the forgiving hands of God, we have taken a major step toward healthy, normal living once more. In truth, there is little we can do about the people and events of yesterday's agony except entrust them to the God of all our tomorrows.

Acceptance

If the first strains of God's song of restoration intone forgiveness, then you can rest assured the connecting bridge of the melody will be acceptance. In learning about dying and passing the lessons on to me my mother lived the best, most profound moments of her life. I will remember her for the many years of delightful things she gave me, but I will remember her most for her attitude of acceptance toward her death during her last seven weeks.

I have prayed that I will be able to teach those same God-given attitudes of acceptance to my children even before it is time for me to keep my appointment with death. I have been working on it for many years and of course continue to do so now, when cancer hangs as a dark cloud above my head.

Fear and denial are at the opposite end of the world from acceptance, and I had to face this fact when I began to teach my children about death and dying. I wish I'd started out earlier with Rick and Laurie, but like every other parent in the world, I felt they would know soon enough about death's dark curtain. I thought, *Why bring it up?* Death, however, whether we like it or not, is a vital part of living; and we need to understand that preparation and discussion of this almost taboo subject will be of great value to our children as they mature into their adult lives.

Based on many other people's stories and my own observations, I think that children should be included in conversations about dying both before and after a death has occurred. They should be allowed to hear the funeral plans and decisions that are being made. It's not a time for hustling them outside or for stopping conversations about "Grandma" (who just died) when they enter a room. We need to let them listen to our grief and see our tears because that lets them know their own grief and tears are not abnormal. We adults need to be sensitive to the fact that they are feeling sad, too. To include them in our discussions and to be available to answer their questions helps them allow the work of mourning to take place. Children have just as big a need to come to closure as adults do, but they need to be able to express their sadness and their guilt (if they have any, whether based on real or imagined wrongdoing) and be given a chance to work through it.

I once viewed a TV special called "The Right to Die." On the program, Dr. Elisabeth Kübler-Ross stated that she felt people must be able to accept death and its processes at least by the time they are twenty years old. She stated that if they had not accepted death by their young adulthood, then it would be very hard for them later to cope with it.

Years ago my family had quite a discussion about accepting death. We talked about the "what ifs" of dying: What if Dad died? What if Mom died? What if you died? What would you want for your funeral? And the conversation which started during dinner went on long after dinner was finished. I will always remember the discussion because for some strange reason everyone waxed hysterically witty and yet some serious statements were made that night that will be remembered and carried out when we die.

It was at that dinner I learned who in my family did not want an open casket. ("If that lid is open I'm going to reach up during the middle of the service and pull it down over me! I don't want everybody staring down and saying, 'My, my, doesn't he look natural!'") I also found that my family wanted me to dress in powder blue at each one's funeral— not black as I had imagined. (Rick said prophetically, "Well, I hope no one phones to console Mother after someone in this family has died, because she won't be home. Mom'll be out shopping for a blue dress!")

We agreed that night that we would all want a memorial service in our church rather than in a mortuary. We wanted songs like "When Morning Gilds the Skies," "How Great Thou Art," and "Blessed Assurance" to be sung. I particularly wanted flowers—tons of flowers; none of this, "In lieu of flowers, please send money to . . ." I remembered that at my mother's funeral, when I could no longer bear to study her beloved face, I looked around her casket, and my heart found refuge and great comfort in the hundreds of floral bouquets. Yes—I want flowers.

While we laughed and loved a great deal that night, we took some serious steps toward firming up in all our hearts, not just my children's, the acceptance of death as a part of living. I concluded that the definition of my funeral should be: "a Christian worship service to God in loving memory of the one who had died."

In teaching our children the acceptance of the death process, we must also work on our own acceptance. Nothing facilitates our acceptance of the eventuality of death faster than making out a will.

Frankly, I never did think too much about making out a will. When I was in my forties I felt that I was too young to bother with it, and so procrastinating seemed to be the best plan. Also, since I knew I'd probably spend or give away most of what was allotted to me financially during my lifetime, I really didn't think there would be too much left to divide.

That's how I felt before I read a powerful message in Catherine Marshall's book *To Live Again*: "Peter . . . had left no will." It was in those few printed pages that Catherine Marshall related the horror she endured after her husband died leaving no will. After reading it, my husband and I came to a decision: We would make out a will immediately. And we did.

Our education escalated considerably after I learned what happens to property and things after death. I discovered that if at the time of death there is no written, valid will, the *state chooses* the beneficiaries of all *your* properties—and the state's decisions are absolutely final. I also learned that many, many Christians (something like eight out of ten) at that time did not have wills; and sadly, out of the few Christians who did make wills, almost fifty percent did not remember the Lord's work or their home church in whatever they left behind.

Some of the bereaved I've talked with have been stumbling down dark, discouraging corridors for years because of the confusion that occurred when there was no will. Any money the survivors may have thought they had was used up in probate taxes or went to state funds. Having no will produced one financial headache after another for them. Any degree of acceptance of death is next to impossible to the person left with these overwhelming financial burdens. To experience the agonies of settling an estate (even a very small one) is to experience frustrations of great magnitude.

Should the day come when our children must decide what to do with our possessions, we need to have left them with a clear, valid will to direct them. The financial value of our estates may not be great, but the peace of mind for our families and the knowledge that our money will go where *we* want it helps nudge us out of denial of our unavoidable death and into a healthy acceptance of the dying process.

We encourage acceptance not only by freely discussing death with our families and by making sure there is a valid will, but by one other important way as well: by understanding those five stages of death and dying I wrote of earlier.

Remember them?—denial, anger, bargaining, depression, and finally, acceptance. The dying go through these stages and so do those standing by. The time of bereavement will probably reinstate the stages. Let's not be impatient or discouraged; remember the ultimate goal of these stages is acceptance.

Karen was a young woman who worked her way through those stages to acceptance. Six months before she died she said to one of our pastors, "Keith, whatever time I have left . . . I'm not going to leave sad, grief-stricken memories, but by the grace of God, I'm going to leave happy, victorious times and memories for my family." And so she did! But, like her family and those of us who are left behind, we must remember that these difficult stages raise their ugly heads many times before we reach acceptance and many months after we think we are over them.

As I was writing this manuscript the first time, my daughter, Laurie, eighteen at the time, read my typed carbon copies of the first seven chapters, and then she wrote me the following letter. In part, it says:

> My precious Mother,
>   I love you dearly, and after reading Mourning Song, I had to face the fact that someday I will have to say goodby to you . . . as you had to say goodby to your precious mother.
>   After reading the book I asked God to take you quickly when you are to "keep your appointment." But then, the more I thought about it, the more my mind changed. . . . You see, you learned so much from your mom and she left you with some of the most precious as well as valuable lessons because she died slowly. I want to learn all I can from you now, but I also want to gain a whole different area when you die. Not only do I feel this about you, but about Daddy, too.
>   To be honest, though, I don't want you to die at all. But because of your book, I think your death will be a little bit easier. Thank you for your book, Mom . . . I needed it!
>
>   Love,
>   Laurie

Acceptance, standing on its shaky, newborn legs, began to live in Laurie's heart. When death strikes at me or anyone in our family, I believe Laurie will have a giant head start in hearing the message and melody of acceptance.

A friend of mine stood by his father's casket and then wrote these brief lines. Out of his pen flowed his acceptance song:

> that which gave me life
> lies before me lifeless.

the voice—the Golden Tenor—
reposes—forever silent.

but is it?

perhaps in that Mysterious Realm
a new voice is heard
to challenge the beauty of
celestial choirs.

perhaps
he who laughed so easily,
who lived life and
lived it with such gusto, and
who was at one equally with
peasants or kings
this very moment
has audience with
the King of Kings.

earth is poorer now—
yet richer
for having known him.

Hope

If God's restoration song begins with forgiveness, then bridges into the melody of acceptance, it is the incredible finale of hope that brings us up out of our seats to applaud and shout, "Yes!"

God gives hope in many ways and one of his better ways is with the poetry that he writes through the pens of his people. As I look back now, I can see that just before I experienced the deaths of my son, grandfather, and mother God was tuning up the orchestra for his song of hope. Only a scant two months before David died, my friend Al Sanders introduced me to the prose and poems of Martha Snell Nicholson. What seemed then like a casual remark by Al ("Joyce, you'll love her poems") turned out to be far more accurate than he or I imagined.

I don't believe in coincidences, and I can see in retrospect that God deliberately worked through Al Sanders and turned my heart to Martha's writings. One thing that made her poems special to me was that she wrote all of them while confined to her bed. She had been ill for twenty-five years with five major diseases, including cancer. She also had lost her father and Howard, her much-beloved husband. But her writings were special for another reason. They were not blissfully ignorant of truth or filled with falsely sweet sayings that try to act like an anesthetic to block our anger, pain, or sorrow. Martha's writings were honest, sometimes blunt, but real; and at the same time they were filled with large measures of hope.

I began to read her work during the dark months of blindly stumbling through my grief while trying to heal physically from my surgery and emotionally from David's death. I had received hundreds of letters which many times included poems. I hate admitting this, but many of them only made me angry. The lights that shone in Martha Snell Nicholson's work were a welcome relief. This poem, "Broken Dreams," really touched me. I suppose the reason it did was that finally someone admitted that my dream *was* broken.

Broken Dreams

I do not hold my broken dreams
And cling to them and weep,
Beseeching God to mend them now.
I give them back to Him
From Whom they came, . . .
And a secret joy lightens all my days.
And long sweet nights I dream
Of how it fares with them in Heaven.

I fill my little day
With little tasks,
I give the best I have
To him who asks.
Years that are full
More quickly pass.

Some day the stars will shine again,
The flowers bloom,
And all the winds blow sweet.
Some day,
In Heaven's golden dawning,
Will tender angels give them back to me,
My broken dreams—unbroken then,
All loveliness,
Complete.

Martha Snell Nicholson

Somehow, because of the hope that was infused in the last five lines, I began to hold steady. I filled my "little day with little tasks" and tried to "give the best I have to him who asks." I did that then and I find I'm doing that now.

After my mother died I received this letter from my friend, Mary Korstjens:

Dearest Joyce,

You and your family are on my mind and heart so much these days.

The book of poems by Martha Snell Nicholson that you lent me once had the two poems I have enclosed. They were very precious to me when my mom went to be with God.

Joyce, may God's love sustain and strengthen you beyond belief.

All my love and prayers,
Mary

One of those poems Mary sent was called, "Along the Golden Streets." It was poignantly beautiful and softly comforted my heart, but the other poem became my theme song over the next years. I still never read it without thinking of the pain-racked, bedridden little woman who stubbornly refused to give in to her own suffering and gave her best by penning:

The Heart Held High

> God made me a gift of laughter
> And a heart held high,
> Knowing what life would bring me
> By and by,
>
> Seeing my roses wither
> One by one,
> Hearing my life-song falter,
> Scarce begun,
>
> Watching me walk with Sorrow. . . .
> That is why
> He made me this gift of laughter—
> This heart held high!
>
> Martha Snell Nicholson

Martha Snell Nicholson also helped me in my concept of what death is really about by this poem:

The Other Side

> This isn't death—it's glory!
> It is not dark—it's light!
> It isn't stumbling, groping,
> Or even faith—it's sight!
> This isn't grief—it's having
> My last tear wiped away;
> It's sunrise—it's the morning
> Of my eternal day!

This isn't even praying—
It's speaking face to face;
Listening and glimpsing
The wonders of His grace.
This is the end of pleading
For strength to bear my pain;
Not even pain's dark mem'ry
Will ever live again.

How did I bear the earth-life
Before I came up higher,
Before my soul was granted
Its ev'ry deep desire,
Before I knew this rapture
Of meeting face to face
The One who sought me, saved me,
And kept me by His grace!

In her writings I discovered that Mrs. Nicholson lived in a hope-filled acceptance of life *and* dying. She lived not in denial, anger, bargaining, or depression, but in reality about her sufferings. I loved her work the most when she wrote, shortly after the death of her husband:

Teach Me to Walk Alone

I live now in a strange new land
Where I must walk alone,
Where I must smile without a tear,
And grief must make no moan.

My comfort and my guiding star,
My tower of strength, has gone.
No peace descends to me with dusk,
No light breaks with my dawn.

The habit of his loving heart
Was thoughtfulness for me.

And yet that heart has ceased to beat . . .
Lord, how can such things be?

My arms have found if they reach out
They clasp but empty air;
And though I search the silent rooms
I never find him there.

I had to learn to walk, dear Lord,
When I was young and small.
Teach me again, for of myself
I can do naught at all!

Our hearts are mended by poetry, especially the honest, valid work borne out of real heartaches and matured by God's direction. Our souls are also healed by prose writings and songs. God used Dr. Elisabeth Kübler-Ross's writings as well as other secular and Christian books to help me find my way. It seemed as always, God led me to books (sometimes only a paragraph or two) which spoke directly and decisively to me and my particular needs.

I believe, though, the strongest writing I found, the source with the most hope, was God's Word. The passage in the New Testament where Jesus is talking to Martha was particularly great in producing hope within me. Remember it? To his friend Martha Jesus laid on the line our steadfast position as Christians on hope and life after death when he said:

> I am the one who raises the dead and gives them life again. Anyone who believes in me, even though he dies like anyone else, shall live again.
>
> John 11:25

These powerful words transform "I *guess* so," I *hope* so," and "I *wish* so," into "I KNOW SO!"

The vigor and vitality of Jesus' words fill in the missing parts in the musical arrangement of our mourning song. John picks up the refrain when he writes:

> And what is it that God has said? That he has given us
> eternal life, and that this life is in his Son. So whoever
> has God's Son has life; whoever does not have his Son,
> does not have life.
>
> 1 John 5:11–12

So, if we know the Lord and are believers, children of God, then we have been guaranteed life, not just here, but forever. This hope separates the men from the boys, the women from the girls; we, who have Christ, can look death, dying, and sorrow right on, eyeball-to-eyeball, and not flinch. Death is ugly, and it is repulsive, but it is not, I repeat, *not* able to bring the life of a Christian to a dreadful, screeching halt. God has worked out an alternate plan, and it is a hope-filled plan. It's a plan that sends our hearts soaring sky high with hope!

When Bernie D. Zondervan died, his well-established Christian publishing house printed many of the letters that were received from people all over the world. I was very inspired as I read them. Here are only two exerpts, but because of the hope they contain I think you might enjoy them. Perhaps they will provide you with a measure of hope in your own circumstances.

I know you [Pat Zondervan, Bernie's brother] see the blessings in the experience. You have told us often of Bernie's faith. You shared with us the Christian convictions concerning the joy and gain which now are his. But nevertheless death for the moment is disruptive. Earthly ties are precious and they don't break easily. Moreover, I think you two brothers were unusually close. But the thing which made you close was your mutual service of the Lord. That goes on. Bernie's in heaven and yours on this earth. And one day you will be reunited in glory. I like John 14:3. I think it is Christ's description of the death of a Christian. "I will come again." The Lord took Bernie. Not cancer, not weakness. Nothing but the Lord. That is most comforting. "And receive you unto myself." That's what's happened to him. He's with the Lord. All of us here below live by faith. But faith at best is weak. It varies. One day it's rich and strong. The next it's weak and feeble. But Bernie lives now by sight. He's with the Lord. That is far better. We sorrow, but not as the world.

Rev. John A. DeKruyter, Pastor
Seymour Christian Reformed Church

There was a time when I would have expressed my regrets in the learning of Bernie's passing, but that was before I fully understood what he passed INTO . . . and not for the world would I ever wish his presence here, when he has so much of great joy in sharing there—His is by far the better place than that which you and I share today. In some respects, I am sure that I become a bit anxious for the appointed day myself—I hope that you and I can join in a jubilation meeting there soon, together.

Heartsill Wilson
America's Dynamic Voice of Marketing

In the beautiful book *Home Before Dark*, written by Bryant M. Kirkland, there are three sentences which vividly stand out:

The hope of heaven fills a need in modern man in answer to his profound search for meaning in existence.

In an age that says there is no meaning, human nature paradoxically cries out for even more meaning.

Without the hope of heaven human existence loses much of its nerve and significance.

It is this hope of heaven, this shining promise of life after death, that restores our confidence. The lovely confidence I saw in my mother while she was dying began to grow in *my* heart after she died, once I realized what a wealth of restoration was in the Christian's hope.

An army chaplain, Colonel Jack Randles, a man of God, lent me an old book of his—*God's Trombones* by the famous Black author James Weldon Johnson. It's a beautiful collection of sermons by a very forceful, creative, and sensitive man. The chaplain knew that as I read *God's Trombones* I'd get to Johnson's sermon on death. Colonel Randles felt it would give me a brand-new scenario of dying, and in doing that would bring its own unique restoration to my heart. He was right.

As I reread each line even today, I find myself breathing a sigh of thanksgiving to God. I identify with the poem because in its lines someone has cried like I. Someone else has hurt, someone else has tried to fathom the depths of sorrowing, and someone else has succeeded in articulating it on paper. It's done so well I can understand death—yes, even my own— much better now. If you can, read it out loud, as I have done many times. I think you'll find that it reaches out from the printed page and touches you with its intrinsic honesty and biblical authenticity.

Go Down Death

Weep not, weep not
She is not dead;
She's resting in the bosom of Jesus.
Heart-broken husband—weep no more;
Grief-stricken son—weep no more;

Left-lonesome daughter—weep no more;
She's only just gone home.

Day before yesterday morning,
God was looking down from his great, high heaven,
Looking down on all his children,
And his eye fell on Sister Caroline,
Tossing on her bed of pain.
And God's big heart was touched with pity,
With the everlasting pity.

And God sat back on his throne,
And he commanded that tall, bright angel standing at
    his right hand:
Call me Death!
And that tall, bright angel cried in a voice
That broke like a clap of thunder:
Call Death!—Call Death!
And the echo sounded down the streets of heaven
Till it reached away back to that shadowy place,
Where Death waits with his pale, white horses.

And Death heard the summons,
And he leaped on his fastest horse,
Pale as a sheet in the moonlight.
Up the golden street Death galloped,
And the hoofs of his horse struck fire from the gold,
But they didn't make no sound.
Up Death rode to the Great White Throne,
And waited for God's command.

And God said: Go down, Death, go down,
Go down to Savannah, Georgia,
Down in Yamacraw,
And find Sister Caroline.
She's borne the burden and heat of the day,
She's labored long in my vineyard,
And she's tired—
She's weary—
Go down, Death, and bring her to me.

And Death didn't say a word,
But he loosed the reins on his pale, white horse,
And he clamped the spurs to his bloodless sides,
And out and down he rode,
Through heaven's pearly gates,
Past suns and moons and stars;
On Death rode,
And the foam from his horse was like a comet in the sky;
On Death rode,
Leaving the lightning's flash behind;
Straight on down he came.

While we were watching round her bed,
She turned her eyes and looked away,
She saw what we couldn't see;
She saw Old Death. She saw Old Death
Coming like a falling star.
But Death didn't frighten Sister Caroline;
He looked to her like a welcome friend,
And she whispered to us: I'm going home,
And she smiled and closed her eyes.

And Death took her up like a baby,
And she lay in his icy arms,
But she didn't feel no chill.
And Death began to ride again—
Up beyond the evening star,
Out beyond the morning star,
Into the glittering light of glory,
Onto the Great White Throne.
And there he laid Sister Caroline
On the loving breast of Jesus.

And Jesus took his own hand and wiped away her tears,
And he smoothed the furrows from her face,
And the angels sang a little song,
And Jesus rocked her in his arms.
And kept a-saying: Take your rest,
Take your rest, take your rest.

Weep not—weep not,
She is not dead;
She's resting in the bosom of Jesus.

James Weldon Johnson

I'm not sure how many times God has used the intriguing message of "Go Down Death" in my life, but he certainly has used it to heal and restore my spirit, as he promised that he'd do in the twenty-third psalm.

Ever since the world began we have been experiencing life and death. The dying part of living will remain with us until God himself calls an end to our existence as we know it.

I think our souls accept the realities of death, the sorrows of grieving, and the living that we must continue to do a little easier if we are willing to listen to God's song of restoration.

The early Christians must have heard the mourning song of God, for we are told that as they were being led to their torturous deaths in the great arena of Rome, they "went to their deaths . . . *singing*." As a singer, I can tell you it's not possible to be scared to death and still sing. The vocal cords restrict into hard, rigid, tautly pulled ropes that will not work. So those martyred Christians had to have heard God's mourning song in their hearts and been filled with his confidence and joy in order to have filled the Coliseum with the sound of their singing.

When you read Jeremiah 31:9, "Tears of joy shall stream down their faces, and I will lead them home with great care," can you see in your mind's eye not only those early Christians, but also all the precious children of God we have lost? Can you see them, those who have gone on before us, standing all together, as if they are being filmed for a great movie spectacular on a supersized screen?—multitude of people, standing there in front of us as our hearts and ears thrill to the stereophonic music pouring out of hundreds of speakers over our souls! Beautifully, as we listen and watch, we can see God leading them *home* with "great care."

Over the picture and above the sound of the triumphant music we hear the narrator. He reads from a script written by Jeremiah, and his resonant words ring deep and clear:

> They shall come home and sing songs of joy upon the hills of Zion, and shall be radiant over the goodness of the Lord. . . . Their life shall be like a watered garden, and all their sorrows shall be gone.
>
> Jeremiah 31:12

But this heavenly throng are not the only ones who can sing the songs of Zion. We who are left can sing, too. We are not suffering from frozen vocal cords that are stiff because of fear, absent because of denial, or tight because of anger and bitterness. Forgiveness, acceptance, and hope have warmed and toned up the flexibility of the vocal cords; and so with full, strong, healthy voices we can sing the songs of hope and restoration!

We can sing the old hymns of the church, like Fanny Crosby's "Blessed Assurance" or Spafford and Bliss's "It Is Well With My Soul" or the song J. A. Crutchfield wrote called "Zion's Hill" with the very boldness and confidence of God. We can sing newer songs like Bill Gaither's "He Touched Me," Audrey Mieir's "Don't Spare Me," or Ruth Harms Caulkin's "But I Do Know" with God's authority giving a reality resonance to our vocal tones. And we can sing songs like this one:

He Giveth More

He giveth more grace when the burdens grow greater,
He sendeth more strength when the labors increase;
To added affliction He addeth His mercy,
To multiplied trials, His multiplied peace.

When we have exhausted our store of endurance,
When our strength has failed ere the day is half done,
When we reach the end of our hoarded resources,
Our Father's full giving is only begun.

His love has no limit, His grace has no measure,
His power no boundary known unto men;
For out of His infinite riches in Jesus
He giveth and giveth and giveth again.

Annie Johnson Flint

We can sing because we know hope and we experience it daily! Because of it we can move, work, and make our time here really count.

My mother wanted me to hear the finale of hope, to be restored by it after she was gone, and then act on it. I know this because in one of her letters to me she wrote:

God bless your ministry, my dear Joyce, I pray your work for Him will be blessed far and wide.

The world needs our testimony in whatever way we are gifted to give it!

Let's be true and press toward God's mark (His plan and purpose for our lives) of the High Calling!

Remember, we have Him and by His life we have life!

So I have listened and heard this remarkable song. The hope of the music creeps over the hills and valleys of my life and heals me and motivates me to action. I can carry on; I can last; I can even *sing* because of the aliveness of God in my soul.

God's powerful, lasting song of restoration opens with a theme of forgiveness and continues into acceptance. It arrives at the chorus and final *coda* with hope, glorious hope, *crescen-*

doing up around us in fully orchestrated, stereophonic sound! It is as we allow our heart and our ears to hear this concluding section of music that God reveals the full-blown beauty of his tender, moving, mourning song.

It is also this part, the hope message of the song, which lingers now in my mind. Long after the song has ended, during those dark, forbidding hours just before dawn, you and I can recall the lyrics and melody line of hope. To our amazement, we can sing the heady, glorious song for whatever life span you and I have left!